Winning Life's Gold Medal

Ten Valuable Life Lessons from the Olympic Games

Gary W. Hall, M.D., OLY

9/20/22

Brook,

Thought you'd

enjoy this,

Best, Bob

Dedicated to my wife, Mary, my children and my grandchildren - the gold medals of my life.

Special thanks go to my friends, Bob Colyer and Alan Bernard, for editing this work. And to all of the Olympians and Paralympians who have dedicated so much of their lives to becoming the best that they can be.

Foreward

I have known Gary Hall Sr most of my life. As an expert for ABC on swimming events during the 1968, 1972 and 1976 Olympic Games, I had a front row seat watching Gary win three Olympic medals in those three consecutive Olympic Games. Twenty years after Gary Sr retired, his son and namesake, Gary Hall Jr, qualified for his first of three consecutive Olympic Games. Gary Jr eventually captured ten Olympic medals, five of them gold.

The Halls' collective accomplishments have made history. They were and still are the only father and son pair to compete in three Olympic Games. Winning an Olympic medal is the ultimate achievement in the sport of swimming. However, the lessons that are learned along the way to the podium bring the most value to a competitor.

No one articulates this better than Gary Hall Sr in *Winning Life's Gold Medal*. As an elite athlete and the father of an elite athlete on the world stage, Gary extracts lessons learned through very specific behind-the-scenes Olympic and other experiences. His life's journey is a brave, open and raw account of how he has survived personal betrayal, pettiness and public family shaming. In eventually discovering his true calling as a coach in his beloved sport of swimming, and as a mentor to athletes, it is the Olympian within him that ultimately shines through.

While offering ten valuable life lessons, based mostly on his Olympic experiences, Gary also seeks redemption and self-discovery. Hopefully, in reading *Winning Life's Gold Medal,* these ten life lessons will help do the same for you.

Donna de Varona
Olympic Gold Medali

Contents

Introduction

Inspired by the Olympians of Ancient Greece and the need for more physical exercise among the children of that era, the Frenchman Baron Pierre de Coubertin created the Modern Olympic Games in the early 1890's. He had more than just an athletic contest in mind.

The five countries that made up the area of Greece during those ancient times from 776 B.C. to the 4th Century A.D. were often at war with each other. However, during the two weeks of the athletic contests held in Olympia every four years, called the Olympic Games, the five countries agreed to a cease fire and co-existed in peace. This two-week period was called the Olympic Truce.

De Coubertin reasoned that if the five warring countries of Ancient Greece could get along peacefully for those two weeks, why couldn't the entire world do the same? If the original Olympic Games inspired world peace for two weeks, why could it not do the same for longer?

Many considered De Coubertin an idealist. Yet, he was clearly a visionary and a man of principles. In developing the Modern Olympic Games, he was faced with incredible obstacles, including two World Wars, near financial ruin, the Nazi attempt to take the Games over to advance their own agenda and countless other people trying to alter its intent. Nonetheless, De Coubertin persevered.

After 120 years, the Modern Olympic Games has evolved into arguably the most popular sporting event in the world. In 1896, at the first modern Olympic Games, 250 athletes (all males) from 14 different countries competed. A few thousand spectators observed. By 2016 in the Summer Olympic Games of Rio de Janeiro, 11,237 athletes (6,178 men and 5,059 women) from over 200 countries competed and 3.6 billion people watched it on television.

For the Olympic Games in Tokyo in 2021 (if it goes forward), there will be 33 sports on the schedule, five more than there were in Rio. There will be 339 gold medals awarded to the Olympic Champions in Tokyo. Less than 3% of the Olympic athletes will have the honor of winning and standing on top of the podium, watching their National Flags being raised to their county's Anthem. Most of those gold medalists will become heroes in their home countries. Many of them become celebrities for life.

The truth is that the vast majority of the athletes competing in the Olympic Games don't have much of a chance of winning any medal at all: gold, silver or bronze. Their goal and life-long dream is to make their Olympic Team, to have the honor of competing for their country. To any athlete in an Olympic sport, winning an Olympic gold medal remains one of, if not the most, coveted prizes of all. Few people can ever get there.

I competed in three Olympic Games of 1968 (Mexico City), 1972 (Munich) and 1976 (Montreal) in the sport of swimming. My oldest son, Gary Jr, also competed as a swimmer in three Olympic Games of 1996 (Atlanta), 2000 (Sydney) and 2004 (Athens). To my knowledge, we are the only father and son to have each competed in three Olympic Games. Collectively, we won 13 Olympic medals (Gary Jr won 10 (5 gold, 3 silver, 1 bronze) and I won 3 (2 silver and 1 bronze)) [1]. I am very proud of our Olympic accomplishments. Winning 13 Olympic medals in one family is not too bad.

My greatest athletic honor came in the Opening Ceremony of the 1976 Olympic Games of Montreal. There, I was elected by my fellow Olympic teammates to carry the U.S. flag and lead our team of over 600 athletes into Montreal Stadium. I was the first swimmer in U.S. history to be selected for that honor. Michael Phelps was the second swimmer to receive that honor in 2016.

From 2005 to 2016, I served as Vice President (2005-2012) and President (2012-2016) of the United States Olympians and Paralympians Association. During my term as President, I am most proud of bringing the Paralympians into our organization. I have never met a more inspiring group of athletes than the Paralympians.

While the Olympic Games have had a profound influence on my life and on the life of Gary Jr, the Olympic Games are far from perfect. In virtually every Olympic Games can be found evidence of bias, corruption, favoritism, racism, cheating and a host of other disturbing qualities. Yet, in spite of all of that, the Olympic Games not

---

[1] In 2019, I was credited with being part of the gold medal relay retroactively by the IOC website Olympic.org for participating in preliminary heats of the men's 4 x 100 medley relay in the 1972 Olympic Games of Munich. From 1984 onward, all members competing on the relays received the medal earned by their team in the finals.

8

only survives, Olympism, a philosophy which embodies the spirit of the Olympic ideals, continues to grow stronger each quadrennium.

There are many Olympic ideals; fair play, hard work, excellence, perseverance, sportsmanship, respect, friendship, peace…just to name a few. While those are all virtuous and desirable qualities, the purpose of this book reaches beyond espousing those ideals, which are woven into the lessons of each chapter. I have been fortunate to see the Olympic Games from many vantage points. As a young Olympic dreamer, an Olympic participant, a father of an Olympian, a brother-in-law of an Olympian, a coach of Olympians and as President of the US Olympians and Paralympians Association, I am somewhat uniquely positioned to have learned some of the most valuable lessons that the Olympic Games and its Olympians and Paralympians have to offer.

The good news is that you don't have to win an Olympic medal or even make an Olympic Team to benefit from these Olympic lessons. They are lessons for everyone who dares to listen. As you read through the ten lessons, rather than considering this being a contest of who can swim or run the fastest, throw the farthest, jump or vault the highest to qualify for an Olympic team, instead, consider this as a contest of living, the way in which you live your life.

Imagine that at the end of your life, before you are too old, decrepit or weak to climb up on a podium, you are to be considered for the honor of winning a gold, silver or bronze medal, depending on how you had lived your life. How would you fare? Would you stand on top of the podium or would you even be invited to the ceremony? How would the judges, or The Judge, score you? Would you be evaluated on the basis of how much you earned or how many you employed? Or how much you gave back to society or to charitable needs? Or on how many people you helped? Or on how good a parent or family member you were? Or on the basis of some new invention, development or idea you created? Or on how much you suffered? Or would you be judged based on some combination of all of the above? Or based on totally different criteria? Who knows? Or do you even care?

There is a lot more at stake in this life contest than an imaginary medal. Even if you don't believe in God or an Almighty Being or Eternal life, there is still a lot at stake. If you don't care about how you live your life on Earth, you will likely become a burden rather than a contributor to the world. You will simply add to the world's turmoil and its people not getting along with each other. I don't think it is even possible for someone that doesn't care about life to be truly happy for any extended period of time. Just to be happier is worth you caring about how you live your life. That is worth all of us caring about how you live your life.

Far be it for me to presume anything or to make any judgments about how you are living your life. What one person perceives as a good deed, another may consider evil. All I know is that in your life, no matter how carefully thought out or considered, even the best made plans go awry. No matter what your vision is of your future, regardless of how much future you have left, no matter how many insurance policies, contracts, exit strategies or hedge funds you devise or participate in, no matter how successful you think you are, at some point in time a bomb will drop into your life. It may have dropped already. The bomb drops in everyone's life, often several times. An unexpected death, an incurable disease, a pink slip, a divorce, a bankruptcy, an accident, a lawsuit, COVID; at least one awful and unexpected thing will happen to you or one of your family members that will knock you flat on your back.

When the bomb goes off in your life, what next? Unfortunately, it may not be until that bomb drops that you stand back and take a good look at your life. It may take that kind of event for you to ask some tough questions: "Am I living the kind of life I expected or wanted? Are all of those things that I once considered so important and such high priorities in my life really that important?"

After a tragic event in your life, will you probably ask yourself the question, "Why did this happen to me?" It may also be the first time in your life that you begin to contemplate your life's true meaning. It may be the first time you consider where on the podium you might end up, or if you deserve to get there at all.

Today, whether we like it or not, the world is changing faster than we can even imagine. Through the internet and social media, information, whether good or bad, true or false, now travels at the speed of light and globally. COVID appeared overnight and suddenly changed all of our lives; some of them drastically. Quarantines, social distancing, infections, deaths, thousands of businesses closing, the toll and aftermath of this viral bomb going off is still unclear.

As a result of COVID and other events occurring in succession, almost like a perfect storm, we now find ourselves with more social unrest, more anger, more fear, more hostility, more criticism, more divisiveness, more concern than I can ever recall in my lifetime. There is a greater division of allegiances to political leaders and parties than ever before, at least in recent history. The criticism by all sides is loud and persistent. The brutality of the policemen in Minneapolis, resulting in the death of George Floyd, broadcast instantly to the world, sparked more social upheaval and unrest than we have seen since the riots of 1968. Even with the Dow Jones Industrial Average stock prices reaching all-time highs, confidence in our future seems to be at an all-time low.

Fifteen years ago, I started this book with the same ten lessons in mind, but never published it. It wasn't the right time. Now it is. The very greatness of our country is being threatened not from the outside, but from within. Our brilliant medical community will find an answer to COVID, but we must find a way to restore peace among ourselves. That part is on us. Ending racism starts with having respect for each other. Our inability to get along, and to have respect for each other's opinions or beliefs, whether we agree with them or not, is now the greatest threat we face as a nation.

From the perspective of an Olympian, I will share with you ten important and tough lessons about life that I have learned from the Olympic Games and my journey to get there. Most of them I have learned not from winning, but from losing races. My hope is that these lessons will inspire you to care and think about the way you are living your life, now and in the future. Call me an idealist, like De Coubertin may have been, or even old-fashioned. It doesn't matter to me.

America became the greatest country of the world not by chance, but by its people holding to some important beliefs, beliefs that are worth keeping. Americans are not perfect by any means, but I really believe that we can turn our country back around. Not economically, but emotionally. We have to, if we are to have a country that our children and grandchildren will be proud of and will want to be a part of.

Lesson One
We all can become Gold Medalists in something

"Everyone has inside of him a piece of good news. The good news is that you don't know how great you can be! How much you can love! What you can accomplish! And what your potential is!" Anne Frank

Of all the lessons in this book, this one may be the most important. While there may be many challenges that we face in our quickly changing world, there are two major ones that stand out:

Challenge #1: Americans have become increasingly critical and intolerant of anyone else's opinion but their own. People are doing more talking (or typing) than listening. They react and respond too quickly, before considering the consequences of their words or actions.

We have always been a nation of bright, independent thinkers. We have always been a nation of people with diverse thoughts and opinions. What has changed is our ability to tolerate any opinion other than our own. Being intolerant of others' opinions is bad for our country.

Mostly through social media, but also on the traditional news media, it is far easier today to criticize, to condemn, to chastise, to castigate and to belittle others than ever before. People do, constantly. In doing so, they instantly reach tens of thousands of people, spewing out vitriol with a few strokes on the keyboard or iPhone, or with a few choice words on television. Others join the bandwagon to continue the spread, sometimes to the extent of becoming viral, reaching millions of people. The result is not only dividing America, it also escalates the anger within its people. Neither one is healthy.

The pen has always been mightier than the sword. While at one time, few of us had pens, today, we virtually all do. Through Facebook, Twitter and other social media, we can quickly write whatever we want, with an almost unlimited audience. The rules have changed.

At the 2000 US Olympic Trials in Indianapolis, long before Facebook and Twitter, Gary Jr qualified for the Olympic Team in the 50 meter and 100 meter freestyle events. While Gary had been one of the best 100 meter freestylers in the world since the 1994 World Championships, the fact that he even made the Team in this event surprised many people.

One year before those Trials, Gary had been diagnosed with Type 1 Diabetes. It took months for him to come out of his funk from the diagnosis. Then it required several more months to get back into serious training, once his blood sugar was under control.

The fact that he was training for the Olympic Games at all with Type 1 Diabetes was remarkable, but if he were to attempt this feat of making another Olympic Team, he and his coach, Mike Bottom, decided it would be best to try for one event only, the 50 meter sprint. No swimmer with Diabetes had ever qualified for an Olympic Team before.

He was paving new ground. He only had about six months to get ready, so he decided to train only for the sprint event.

In the Spring of 2000, at the very last qualifying meet for the Olympic Trials, The Janet Evans Invitational in Los Angeles, Mike had a change of heart. On the final day of the meet, he decided that it would be better for Gary to swim the 100 freestyle at the Trials. He would not be expected to make the Team in that event, but instead, he would use it as a warm-up race before the 50 meter sprint. By using it as warm-up race and getting a race under his belt, he might do better in the sprint.

Gary had not swum a 100 freestyle race in competition for nearly two years. Mike had Gary lead off the 4 x 100 freestyle relay team, so his time would become official. He squeezed under the cutoff time by .1 second. He would get to swim the 100 meter freestyle on the second day of the Trials, helping prepare for the 50 sprint.

At the Olympic Trials in Indianapolis, having one of the slowest entry times for the 100 meter freestyle, Gary was seeded in the very first heat of the preliminaries. I am not sure how he did it, but he managed to drop his entry time by about 3 seconds in that heat, qualifying easily for the semi-finals.

From there, Gary dropped even more time to make the finals. On the following evening, he placed second to Neal Walker, qualifying for the Olympic Team in the 100 meter freestyle event, placing him automatically on the 4 x 100 freestyle relay. He was ecstatic.

Not only did Gary shock everyone by making the Team in the 100 freestyle, his teammate and training partner, 19-year-old Anthony Ervin, also qualified for the relay team. The four American men who would be swimming on that freestyle relay in Sydney looked to be invincible. The American team had never lost this relay in the entire history of the modern Olympic Games. It seemed as if they would keep the tradition going.

After the Trials, Gary was asked to write a blog for NBC.com, leading up to the Olympic Games. In his excitement and anticipation for the forthcoming freestyle relay race with the Australian team, he wrote the following:

"My biased opinion says that we will smash them like guitars. Historically, the U.S. has always risen to the occasion. But the logic in that remote area of my brain says it won't be so easy for the United States to dominate the waters this time."

The Australian sports media took a few words from that statement, *'we will smash them like guitars'*, and printed it over and over again. It was posted on the locker room walls at the Australian training facility. Their coaches used it to stoke the fire inside the four Aussie swimmers. It worked. Gary was a most-wanted-man *down under.*

When the two teams marched out for the finals of the 4 x100 freestyle relay on September 16, the first night of the Olympic swimming competition in Sydney, the raucous home crowd of 17,000 spectators stood on their feet. Australian VIPs, like golfer Greg Norman, were there among them. They all knew about the guitar smashing.

The Americans looked poised, confident and relaxed; perhaps too relaxed. The Aussies looked serious and determined. Ian Thorpe, the great Australian swimmer, was the last swimmer to walk onto the deck, as he needed to change his swimming suit at the final moment. He tore the suit he planned to use trying to hurriedly get it on. Mary and I sat so high up in the nose-bleed section of the stands, we could watch the race better by viewing the large screen television hanging from the ceiling inside the natatorium. We were feeling rather nervous, like we had walked into a bar just before a big fight was about to break out.

Leading off the Australian team was Michael Klim, a world class butterflier and freestyler. Going against him in the next lane was Anthony Ervin, the young talented Californian, who had never been tested on this big of a stage before. As young and inexperienced as he was, Anthony was not the type of swimmer who would back down.

On the start, Klim used his powerful dolphin kicks underwater to surge ahead. When Anthony broke out on the surface, he was looking at Klim's waist. Anthony swam valiantly to try to catch Klim, but never could. Klim touched the wall in a new World Record time of 48.18 on his lead off leg. Ervin swam a very fast 48.89, but the Americans were still .71 seconds behind the Australians.

Once Klim handed over the lead to Australia's second swimmer, Chris Fydler, and for the remaining three legs of the relay, the lead changed hands between the Australian team and the American team seven times. Seven times in eight laps!

The three remaining Americans, Neil Walker, Jason Lezak and Gary, were faster sprinters and would get ahead by the 50 meter mark. Then the Australians would catch them again and pass them just before the finish of their leg.

Finally, when Australian Ashley Callus handed over a small lead of .25 seconds to Thorpe, it would come down to the final leg. With Gary's amazing speed, he built a sizable lead over Thorpe by 50 meters. It looked like Team USA would prevail. Thorpe or *Thorpedo,* as the Australians liked to call him, had a massive kick and finish.

With ten meters to the wall, Gary's inability to train properly for the100 meters because of the diabetes began to show. He was struggling to hang on. Thorpe just kept upping the kick, as if he had two Mercury motors behind him. I have never in my life been in a venue, even a rock concert, that was so loud. Everyone in the stadium was on his feet screaming. Thorpe passed Gary on the very last stroke and touched the wall .19 seconds ahead of him with a new World Record. Both teams were well under the old World Record. The crowd went berserk.

On deck, the three Australians, Klim, Fydler and Callus, played air guitars, taunting the American swimmers, and especially Gary. Nonetheless, in spite of having to eat his words, Gary remained a good sport. Klim recalled the following:

"Hall was the first swimmer to come over and congratulate us. Even though he dished it out, he was a true sportman."

In the post-race press conference, Gary, who always felt his words were taken out of context, said the following:

"I don't even know how to play the guitar. I consider it the best relay race I've ever been part of. I doff my cap to the great Ian Thorpe. He had a better finish than I had."

Years later, one of the American Olympic swimming coaches, Mark Schubert, confided in me by saying:

"Our team was feeling pretty down after losing that relay. When we went back to the Village, we called a team meeting of both the men's and women's Teams together. Things could have easily spiraled downhill from that night on, but they didn't. Your son got up at the meeting and said, 'We may have lost a battle tonight, but we didn't lose the war. We will come back.' He helped turned it around."

After losing the relay that night, the American swimmers made one of the most courageous comebacks in Olympic history. Gary ended up winning the bronze medal in the 100 meter freestyle, ahead of Michael Klim. Anthony and Gary tied for the gold medal in the 50 meter freestyle sprint.[2] The American men won the 4 x100 medley relay on the final night in world record time, getting in the last unwritten word. Gary swam the anchor freestyle leg.

Bob Costas interviewed the members of the gold-medal-winning medley relay team in the NBC tent outside the swimming stadium. Gary was nowhere to be found, so only three of the Americans were present. I looked for him

---

[2] Gary repeated as Olympic gold medalist in the 50 meter sprint in 2004 and Anthony repeated as Olympic gold medalist in the 50 meter sprint in 2016.

outside the natatorium and found him lying on the grass, almost incoherent. I frantically called Dr. Peters. By the time she came and checked his blood sugar, it was 19 (normal levels are 70-130). After sipping some orange juice, he came back to life.

A few choice words taken the wrong way can start a war. It has never been easier to get information, but never harder to get the truth than it is today. Even information that may be true, delivered in snippets, is easily misinterpreted. It is an information *free-for-all* out there.

What does all of that have to do with winning gold medals? Every single human being that is brought into this world has some special gifts or talents. Every single one. We often forget that. We all have the potential to win a gold medal in something. We all have the potential to get better.

Rather than seeking out the good in people, we are doing the opposite. We are looking for the bad. We are inciting anger, dividing instead of uniting.

Challenge #2: Society has perpetuated the myth that we, as Americans, should love and embrace the way we are.

Famous basketball coach, Jim Valvano, once said: *"No matter what business you're in, you can't run in place or someone will pass you by. It doesn't matter how many games you've won."*

I know of no Olympians who ever think they are good enough the way they are. They constantly strive to get better.

Besides, if we all have faults, which we do, how can we ever possibly expect to improve ourselves with that kind of philosophy? We can't and won't.

Fortunately, we are all different. Our world would not be so good if we all had talent for the same thing. We don't. As a result, our world improves and expands in multiple directions at the same time. The key is to figure out where we are talented, and then to nurture and develop that talent.

My wife, Mary, and I have six children. Some were phenomenal swimmers. One was an Olympic Champion. Others became great teachers, or artists or a videographer or a travel agent. The point is, they each have different and unique talents. They each have the potential to win a gold medal in something.

The moment we are satisfied with the way we are is the same moment that we stop improving. That thought or time should never occur and the process of improving in some aspects of our lives should never end.

Here are five ways in which you can change your life today and help solve these two big challenges:

1. **Look for the good in people, not the bad. As Christ teaches us in the Gospel according to St. Luke:** *Do not judge, and you will not be judged;*

do not condemn, and you will not be condemned; forgive, and you will be forgiven. Luke 6:37

2. When you find something that you love to do and are passionate about it, nurture your talent for it. Once you identify what others are good at, complement them. Nurture their talent.

3. When you find something or someone you don't like or agree with, particularly while on Social Media, count to ten before responding. Or perhaps better, refrain from responding at all. Often, it is better to listen than speak. If you do respond, count to 100 before hitting *send.* You might change your mind.

4. Never forget the words of Evelyn Beatrice Hall. "I do not agree with what you have to say, but I'll defend to the death your right to say it." Respect other's opinions, whether you agree with them or not.

5. Never be completely satisfied with the way you are. Always strive to get better.

Lesson Two
Life includes both a Sprint and a Pentathlon

"Happiness is not a matter of intensity but of balance and order and rhythm and harmony." – Thomas Merton

This may be the hardest lesson of this book for you to grasp. For each of us, life should be divided into two segments; the sprint phase and the pentathlon phase. For those who live to be over 100 years of age, I suppose life could also be considered to be a marathon.

When you are young, you have the opportunity to be a sprinter. You can afford to try to win the gold medal in one event, in whatever event you have found that you have talent. A sprinter focuses on one event; one distance. If you want to be the fastest in the world, then you take all of your God-given talent and spend about eight hours per day training for that event. The rest of the time is spent eating, sleeping or visualizing winning the event. There is virtually no other time for anything else in your life. Any time spent on anything else which distracts you from reaching your goal of winning the gold medal, may just be enough to lose it.

During the sprint phase of your life, your gold medal quest may have nothing to do with sports. It could be to get into an Ivy League school, or write a play or a song or a novel, or play a musical instrument, or climb a professional career ladder, or make a lot of money, or get into medical or law school or a million other goals. Whatever the goal, the reason you can afford to go for it when you are young is that, by and large, someone else (usually your parents) is fulfilling your basic needs. Your home, your bed, your food, your tuition; pretty much all of your needs are provided for you. For a brief time in your life, if you choose, you can afford to go *all in* for the gold medal; to become the best that you can be at something.

At some point in life's journey, all of that changes. You get married or find a partner. You start a family and find schools for your children. You get a job or start a new business. You buy a house or a condo. You move into the community, perhaps joining a club. You join a church or find your religion. You pick a charity or cause to get behind. All or most of these choices happen to you within a relatively short period of time. All of a sudden, you realize you are no longer a single-event person. You are no longer training for the sprint. Now you find yourself in a new event, life's pentathlon.

The pentathlon of life is like the Modern Pentathlon, the women's Heptathlon or the Decathlon of the Olympic Games. The Modern Pentathlon includes five events, shooting, running, swimming, fencing and equestrian. The women's Heptathlon involves performing seven different events: 200 meter and 800 meter runs, 100 meter hurdles, high jump, shot put, long jump and the javelin. The Decathlon in track and field requires ten events: 100 meter dash, 400 meter run, 1500 meter run, high jump, pole vault, discuss, shot put, high hurdles, long jump and the javelin. The pentathlon of life is comprised of five different events: faith, family, profession, community and health.

The unofficial title of *the world's greatest male and female athlete* is given to the winner of the Olympic Decathlon and Heptathlon, not to one of the incredible superstars of professional sports, like Michael Jordan, LeBron James, Diana Taurasi, Cheryl Miller, Tom Brady or Wayne Gretzky. As incredible as each of those athletes are or were, they were not considered the world's greatest. That honor always goes to the winner of the Decathlon and Heptathlon.

In either the Modern Pentathlon, Heptathlon or the Decathlon, the winners are not the best in the world in any one of the single events of their sport. To win in the Heptathlon or Decathlon, the athletes must be very good in all events, not just one or two. They have to show great ability in a sprint (100 meter dash) and the endurance for longer running events (400 meter, 800 meter and 1500 meter runs), which require very different skills. They need to have strength for the shot put, discus and javelin and explosiveness for the high jump, long jump and pole vault. The point is that all of these events require very different skills, yet to win the Decathlon or Heptathlon gold medal, one cannot afford to be really weak in any single one of them. The same is true with the pentathlon of life.

I have the honor of knowing some of our greatest Olympic Decathletes; Dan O'Brien, Dave Johnson and Bill Toomey. I can vouch for the fact that their title of *world's greatest athlete* is well-deserved. Dave Johnson was so dominant in the *Superstars Contest,* where he competed against professionals of many other sports, that they finally had to ban him from competing. He won every year he was in the contest.

I discussed with Dan O'Brien how he prepared for the 1996 Olympic Games, where he won the gold medal. In training for the decathlon, Dan would spend some time training on each of the ten events every week, but not every day. And although the training might be adjusted on a daily basis, depending on injuries or fatigue, for the most part, he would spend more time on his weaker events than he would on his stronger events. Knowing that he had more points to gain in the weaker events, he would focus most of his training effort there. However, he would never neglect his strong events.

In the pentathlon of life, most people do just the opposite. They spend most of their time in their comfort zone, training for the events in which they may excel, while sorely neglecting the ones in which they are weak. Most often, the event in which they overindulge is their profession. They still want to try to win the gold medal in that one. They want to be the very best in their chosen profession in the world -- number one.

It seems like an admirable goal. People tend to rationalize their neglect of the other four events by believing that if they are a great provider, if they can buy a bigger house or a fancier car, then their wife or husband and children will somehow understand why they didn't spend more time with them. Somehow, all those great toys and comfortable things will justify them not being there for them when really needed. As for health, most believe that they can always get their health back when they start going to the gym or pool, just as soon as the business gets stabilized and they can hire that manager. As for the community and charity, most people believe that they will start to make donations just as soon as they make their first million. The problem is, they almost never do. As for faith, most people really only seem to need it after the bomb drops in their life. Too often, they wait until they are just about to hit rock bottom before asking for some help.

Though you may be excelling in your profession, if you are neglecting two, three or four of your other events in life's pentathlon, you will never win the gold medal. In fact, you may be doing so poorly in some of those neglected events that they begin to fall apart. That means you score a zero. That's is exactly what happened to Dan at the 1992 Olympic Trials, when he missed on his opening pole vault height. Dan was out of the competition. Reebok had billed the Olympic battle between two titans, Dan and Dave Johnson. But it was not to be. He was finished (at least for that Olympics). Neither he nor Reebok was too happy about that.

The good news is that you have likely not yet scored a zero on any of your neglected events. Even if your scores in those events have been really low, it is never too late to build them back up. It is never too late to redirect your focus in life. In fact, if you really believe that life is a pentathlon, if you really want to have any hope of standing on life's podium, you have to get better scores on your weak events. You have to learn to balance your efforts, even if it means giving up the chance to win the gold in your chosen profession or any other single event. To stand on the podium, you must become good at everything (Faith, Family, Profession, Community and Health), but not necessarily the best at anything.

You can never afford to stand completely still or be totally satisfied with the way you are in life. During the sprint phase of your life, you should be constantly striving to improve your primary event. During the pentathlon phase of life, you must constantly be shifting your focus and energy on the five different events.

That is not to say all five events demand equal time and attention. They don't. The demand for your time and energy for each event will change throughout your life, depending on your age and your circumstances. Don't forget that at some point, your life needs to transition from a sprint to a pentathlon. Then you have five events to worry about, not just one.

Here are five recommendations on how you can improve your scores in the pentathlon of life:

1. **Faith. Don't wait until the bomb drops in your life. Keep your faith every day and don't be afraid to ask God for help. We cannot do everything on our own.**

2. **Family. Faith and Family need to be the number one and two priority in your life. If they are not, rearrange your focus. Make them the most important. Everything else will follow.**

3. **Profession. Try to find something you love doing to make your living. The more you can serve others in your profession, the happier you will be. Be passionate about your profession,**

but not to the extent that you neglect the other four events of your pentathlon.

4. Community. Get involved with your community, regardless of your age. Your community needs you and you need it. Pick your favorite event, charity or cause. Be a contributor of your time, your talent, your money or all of it, but give back to your community. Help make it better.

5. Health. You must make time for this one every week. You need a steady dose of sleep, good nutrition and some exercise on a regular basis to stay healthy. Don't go overboard, though. You are no longer trying to make the Olympic Team. Without having good health, the other four events won't do well.

Lesson Three
We all have a Russian judge in our lives

"The best revenge is to be unlike him who performed the injury." – Marcus Aurelius

Some of you may be too young to remember much about the cold war, but for my entire life, there has always been tension between Russia and America.: the Iron Curtain, the Cuban Missile Crisis and Bay of Pigs with JFK, the nuclear arms race, the race for space, the Russian invasion of Afghanistan resulting in the U.S. boycott of the 1980 Olympic Games, the Russian meddling in Syria and Ukraine, and most recently, the considerable likelihood of the Russians tampering with our Presidential election. These are just some examples of the events that have incited some enormous outrage among Americans toward Russia.

The truth is, whether it is Russia or China or some other country, America always performs better with a competitor or, to some extent, an adversary. Russia has filled that role pretty well most of the time. Olympians are the same. Who can forget the 1980 *Miracle on Ice* hockey match between Team USA and the Red Machine of Russia?

In the 1994 World Swimming Championships in Rome, Gary Jr qualified for the first international meet of his life. The reigning Olympic Champion and World Record holder in his two events, the 50 meter and 100 meter freestyle, was from Russia -- Alexander Popov. In the 1992 Olympic Games of Barcelona, as a young 19-year old swimmer, Popov defeated the reigning *King of Sprints*, American Matt

Biondi, in both of his signature events. Now, Popov was being called the *Czar of Sprints*.

The *Ready Room* is a small enclosed room where all eight swimmers who have qualified for the finals must report for several minutes, before being marched out to the starting blocks for their race. It is an ideal space for mind games to be played. It is the ideal location for psychological warfare. Popov already had a reputation of playing those mind games with his competitors.

When Gary Jr walked into the *Ready Room* for the finals of the 50 meter freestyle, it was the first time he had ever swum against Popov. He sat down in an empty chair with Popov seated directly across the small room facing him. Popov immediately began staring down Gary with his penetrating eyes.

"You are a loser," Popov announced to Gary, loud and clear. Gary did not respond.

"You come from a family of losers", he continued. "Your father was a loser. He never won an individual Olympic gold medal. You are a loser, too."

Gary just sat in silence, staring back at him.

Thus, started the rivalry between the two sprinters, Russian and American, that would last through three more Olympic Games. There was no love between them.

Popov won in Rome and again in Atlanta in 1996, but after that, Gary Jr brought the title of *King of Sprints* back to

America by winning the 50-meter sprint gold medals in the 2000 and 2004 Olympic Games. The *Czar* was taken down. There has never been a fiercer rivalry in the sport of swimming.

In the Olympic Games, no one is supposed to count the medals won by each country, yet everyone does. Russia and the USA are always competing to see which country wins the most Olympic medals. China has now joined the contest. It is sort of an unofficial competition to see who has the best athletes. Not unlike in Ancient Greece, the country that wins the most medals has some bragging rights.

After the Russian doping scandal broke in 2015, where authorities uncovered a systematic scheme of doping Russian athletes, established from the very top of the Russian government on down, it was clear their approach to the Olympic Games was *win at any cost*. China has never been good about playing by the rules, either. Even when I knew other athletes were cheating, I was always glad to compete in a sport where the winners were determined by a clock, rather than a Russian judge.

In watching the Winter Olympic Games, it seems that whenever the American figure skaters compete, for example, they get low scores from the Russian judge. Why? Well, there could be a number of possible reasons. Here are just a few of them:

1. No one back in the Motherland really likes Americans.
2. The Russians feel like they own the sport of skating and no one else has a right to the throne.

3. The Russians don't like the American music that was selected for the skater's routine.
4. The head of the Russian skating federation would no longer invite the judge to the annual banquet where he/she gets all the free caviar and vodka he/she can consume.
5. The judge may get demoted, whereby he/she would no longer get the first-class airfare, hotel accommodations, and limo rides for each Winter Olympics.
6. The judge invested in a new skating arena in Moscow and if the Russian skater doesn't win the gold medal, that means fewer skating lessons for the young Ruskies. That's bad for business.

Whatever the reasons, the Russian judge seems to have an obvious bias against Americans. But, then again, so do the American judges have a bias toward the Russians. If I ever translate this book into Russian, I will have to change the title of the lesson to: We all have an American judge in our lives.

You have a Russian judge in your life, or if not, you will have one. In fact, you may have several. Somewhere lurking out there, often well-disguised, is a person who really doesn't want you to succeed. That is your Russian judge. The bigger and more successful you become, the more Russian judges you will encounter.

The Russian judge in your life doesn't simply want to see you less successful. He or she wants you to fail. The shrewd Russian judge takes great pleasure in plotting and planning your demise. Although it is not always obvious why the Russian judge is going after you, the most common reason is envy. You simply are better than or have accomplished more than he or she ever could. Russian judges don't like that.

Another reason is fear. Through your growth or expansion or success, you may become threatening to the Russian judge. Now, the judge needs to protect his or her turf by going after you.

A third reason is esteem. Particularly when the judge is a young, elected or appointed official, trying to make a name for himself or herself, you become the intended trophy. The bigger you are, the more impressive your head will look mounted up on his or her wall.

As with the skating Russian judge, you may never know the real reason why you are being singled out or targeted. The real question is, once you discover you have a Russian judge in your life, what do you do about it?

As an eye surgeon in Arizona, by the time I discovered my Russian judge, it was too late. I will call him Dr. Z, a physician who had a small practice. Once he managed to become Chairman of the Board of Medical Examiners in Arizona, he became corrupt, abusing his authority and power. He was the Joseph Stalin of Arizona medicine, stripping one physician after another physician of his or her medical license. At a single stroke of his pen, he could end a physician's career, which he often did, until he was finally dismissed for unethical behavior. For me, that was too late.

There were three reasons why the Arizona Medical Board, and specifically Dr. Z, decided to target me. First, my father-in-law was imprisoned as the scapegoat for the S & L debacle and I was associated with his family name, becoming *persona-non-grata*. Second, one of Dr. Z's close friends was an Ophthalmologist who had invited me to join his practice when I first came to town. When I found out that he let his pet cats roam around in his office, I decided to turn him down. My practice grew faster than his did, which did not make him happy. Third, and the most compelling reason, I had the distinction of being the most sued physician in the State of Arizona. That doesn't paint a very good picture of me, but the circumstances around why that happened need an explanation.

In the early 1980's, an entirely new field of Ophthalmology was born, called Refractive Surgery. For the first time, surgeons could correct people's vision so that they would not need to wear glasses any longer. Ironically, the original refractive surgery, called Radial Keratotomy (RK), was developed in Russia by Dr. Svyatoslav Fyodorov. By the mid 1980's, the procedure was becoming very popular in the United States.

By 1986, four years into my practice, I decided to become a refractive surgeon. I learned from one of the best RK surgeons in the world at the time, Dr. Ralph Berkeley of Houston, Texas. Having a good outcome with RK, more than any other procedure I knew, depended greatly on the skill of the surgeon. Cutting precision-like linear incisions with diamond blades on the delicate cornea, a refractive surgeon needed to have bilateral manual dexterity and rock-steady hands. Some surgeons had neither, and still attempted to do RK, resulting in poor outcomes. RK did not enjoy a great reputation in the USA.

The other unusual aspect of RK surgery is that it was almost as much an art as it was a science. Virtually every surgeon developed his or her own technique of performing it. With RK, developing a standard of care was virtually impossible, as two surgeons would not agree on the best of way of doing it.

Nonetheless, many people wanted to be freed from their dependency on using glasses. Good RK surgeons' practices grew quickly. From 1986 to 1994, my RK practice steadily grew to the point that I was operating on thousands of patients each year. I operated on sports legends in auto racing, like Al Unser, Jr, Emerson Fittipaldi, Paul Tracy and Max Papis, whose lives depended on having good vision. When other celebrities began coming to me for surgery, I decided I should double my malpractice insurance from $5 million to $10 million, just to be safe. It was a big mistake. After eight years of doing refractive surgery, I had never been sued for malpractice.

In 1994, that all changed. I will never forget the pit in my stomach the day the process server arrived at my office. One of my RK patients was suing me for malpractice. My immediate response was anger, more like rage, and an urge to fight back. I notified my malpractice carrier, and they put a defense attorney right on the case. We spent weeks preparing for it.

The trial by jury lasted almost a week. It was emotionally exhausting, as their expert witness accused me of doing everything wrong. The jury was not convinced, however, and ruled in my favor. They awarded nothing to the plaintiff. I was relieved.

Six months later, a second lawsuit occurred, as unexpectedly as the first one. Again, weeks of preparation ensued with a week-long trial ending in an award to the plaintiff of $2,500. Compared to what the plaintiff's attorney was asking for, that was a victory.

When a third lawsuit occurred several months after the second, I was totally disheartened. Each one of these trials took its toll on me, emotionally and financially. My insurance carrier apparently felt the same way. The complaints were costly to defend and the standard of care was too vague. They notified me that they would no longer be defending me in these claims and they would exhaust my entire limits of insurance coverage ($10 million) to any and all plaintiffs that filed a malpractice suit against me over the following year. At the end of one year, I would no longer have malpractice coverage, nor could I get any more, even at an exorbitant cost.

When the word got out to the malpractice attorneys in Arizona, they went into a frenzy. I became the *silicone-breast-implant surgeon* equivalent in Ophthalmology. Malpractice attorneys put ads in the paper seeking any patients that I had operated on in the past. It would be the easiest money they would ever make. No preparation. Just file a suit from one of my surgical patients, regardless of when it occurred or what the outcome was, and they would get a big check. The suits came pouring in, sometimes two in one week. By the end of the year deadline, around 75 patients of mine had independently filed a claim against me. Many of them had 20/20 vision with great results. Some of them, very few actually, did not. It didn't matter. Their chances to win this lottery were 100%. After their plaintiff attorneys took their big cut, each patient received about $135,000 just for filing the claim.

It was another lesson in humility and an education in how the system really works. Until I left my practice in 2006, I was never able to get malpractice insurance again. I operated *bare,* assuming all the risks myself. Perhaps I was naïve, even stupid for doing so, but I never got sued again. Not once. There were no deep pockets to go after. During that time, however, the Board of Medical Examiners became vicious in their desire to end my medical career in Arizona.

One time, after pouring through hundreds of surgical charts, an investigator from the Board identified 20 patients' who had undergone refractive surgery that he was certain I had permanently damaged their vision. Dr. Z then had his *expert witness,* an adversarial Ophthalmologist that I knew, review the charts to confirm I had indeed damaged those poor people. Not once did he or his *expert* ever call or contact any of the 20 patients to ask how they thought they (the patients) were doing.

When I was called in for the hearing on these cases, in front of the entire Arizona Medical Board, all 20 identified patients came to testify on my behalf. Some of them drove for hundreds of miles to be there. Turns out, they were all very satisfied with their vision from the surgery. None of them believed that their vision had been damaged. Most of them had 20/20 vision without using glasses. The problem is that none of them were allowed to speak to the Medical Board during the hearing. Dr. Z decided that the only opinion that mattered in these cases against me was the one of his *expert witness*. Not even the patients, the *victims* themselves, were allowed to weigh in.

After being fined and handed a severe penalty by the Board, I walked outside the Board room with my head held high. It was another huge dose of humility, but I was pretending not to appear defeated. I could immediately tell that the patients were infuriated that they were not given an opportunity to be heard. I tried to console them, but they should have been consoling me. I was a mess. Finally, Mary grabbed me by the hand and pulled me away. I was reeling from the pain and embarrassment. She looked me straight in the eyes and said:

"You realize you are doomed, don't you?"

I did. This Board, with Dr. Z leading the charge, was out to get me. Yet, being as stubborn as I am, I kept trying to fight an unwinnable fight in a corrupt system with a corrupt judge and with no due process for a fair trial. For the next ten years, the Medical Board continued to take one small piece of me at a time, until I was finally devoured. My medical career was over.

This story begs the question again. Once you discover who your Russian judge is, do you stay and fight or not? It is not an easy question to answer. Every situation and Russian judge are a bit different. Sometimes it is better to fight and sometimes it is better to walk away.

As Olympians, we are bred to fight, to never give up. That may not always be the right strategy. For ten years, I had a visual image of Dr. Z's head in the bullseye of a dart board, and I was hurling dart after dart right into the bullseye. Today, I have a visual image of him on my *people to thank* bucket list.

Leaving medicine was not a decision that I made. The decision was made for me. It was the best decision I never made. The day I left Arizona, I began a new career as a swimming technique coach, falling back on my Olympic roots once again. I have never been happier and I never looked back.

Often, whether fair or unfair, your Russian judge will significantly alter your life. How you respond to that alteration is up to you. Perhaps, like with me, it will be one of the best things that ever happened to you.

Once you encounter your Russian judge, here are my eight best recommendations on how to deal with the situation:

1. **Is your Russian judge approachable? If so, the most prudent course of action may be to keep your enemies close. Try to become a friend, or if not, at least become someone that the Russian judge has less reason to hate. Send him some caviar and vodka.**

2. Discover the root and cause of your Russian judge's anger. Sometimes the problem is resolvable. Sometimes it is not. It is very hard to solve a problem when you don't know what it is.

3. Before engaging in battle, weigh all of your options. Sometimes the battle is prudent, even necessary. Sometimes it is not. Whether you win or lose, battles always leave scar tissue behind.

4. If you do go to battle, understand your battlefield. Don't be like Butch Cassidy and the Sundance Kid, bursting out from behind the rocks with guns blazing only to encounter the entire Bolivian Army waiting for you. Prepare with the best battle team and plan that you can, but make sure the playing field is level enough to win.

5. Don't use *losing your reputation* as an excuse to go to battle. I know how long it takes to earn a good reputation and I know how fast you can lose it. That is not a good enough reason to go to battle. Win or lose, you can lose your reputation either way in battle. The most important reputation you have is with God and your family. The rest is just for your ego.

6. Recognize that by going to battle, you may never reach the podium in the pentathlon of

life. Battles require tremendous amounts of attention and energy, some to the point of obsession. In battle, you will likely have low scores in faith, family, community and health, even if you save your profession or your reputation.

7. Choose your battles wisely. They will each take their toll on you. You can only fight so many. Make sure that you are fighting for the right reasons and that you will accept the consequences at the end.

8. To avoid a battle, consider that a change of business strategy or even of your profession might not be a bad option. Change is always scary. So is uncertainty. Sometimes you just have to take a leap of faith. You may end up much happier where you land.

Lesson Four
Life is not an individual sport. Life is a team sport.

"I built my talents on the shoulders of someone else's talent. I believe greatness is an evolutionary process that changes and evolves era to era." - Michael Jordan

In the Olympic Games, there are team sports, like basketball and volleyball, and there are individual sports, like swimming, gymnastics and track and field. The truth is that the so-called individual sports are actually team sports as well. While each event of the individual sports is represented by a single person or a group of individuals (a relay), the team interaction and spirit in those sports has a profound impact on each individual athlete's performance. There is no greater example of that fact than what occurred in the 1976 Olympic Games during the swimming competition for men and women.

The Men's Story

On the afternoon of July 18, 1976, one day after the Opening Ceremony of the Olympic Games, James "Doc" Counsilman, our Head coach, called a special meeting for all the men's swimmers and other two coaches inside his small bedroom in the Olympic Village.

We were about to walk across the street to the neighboring Olympic Natatorium for the finals of the first day of swimming competition. The men's 200 meter butterfly was the first event on the program and all three

American men, Mike Bruner, Steve Gregg and Billy Forrester, had qualified among the eight finalists. So did the World Record holder in the event, Roger Pyttel from East Germany, the only man to have ever swum the event under two minutes. He qualified with a time just off his World Record time.

The swimmers in the finals had already taken the bus over to the Natatorium to save their legs and warm up properly for the biggest race of their lives. The rest of us crammed tightly into the coaches' room, eager to hear what they would say on this first and critical day of competition. We all knew how important it would be for the team morale to start these Games out on the right foot.

There was an odd sort of calmness and confidence on this Olympic Team, one like I had never seen or felt before. I had been on plenty of great swimming teams, like the Indiana University teams with Mark Spitz that had won several NCAA Championships. Even with those teams, I never quite experienced the same bonding that had occurred during the four weeks of training camp in Canton, Ohio, leading up to this day in Montreal. Neither had I experienced this kind of camaraderie on the two previous Olympic Teams I was a part of in 1968 and 1972.

This team was special. Considering that a good portion of this Olympic Team was comprised of swimmers from two of the fiercest college swimming rivalries in history, Indiana University and the University of Southern California, that was surprising. For the past decade, those two schools had duked it out at the collegiate championships, where either school had won with the other finishing close behind. The meet often went down to the final relay to determine the winner, with swimmers of one team spitting into the lane of the other, just to rub it in. There was simply no love between those two schools in the water.

How so many swimmers from these two rival schools could possibly come together and bond to form an extraordinarily tight team seemed almost miraculous, yet it happened. From the first day of training camp forward, Steve Furniss (USC) and I (Indiana), who shared duties as Co-Captains, asked every swimmer to send their club and school shirts, hats and swim suits home. From now on, we would be allowed to wear only one brand, Team USA. No swimmer was allowed to even mention his school or club team.

Somehow, over the next four weeks, this group of 26 swimmers united and bonded together incredibly closely under the banner of Team USA. We had some entertaining members on the Team, like John 'Rocket Man' Hencken, who was an engineering student at Stanford. Nearly every day he would launch off his home-made rockets in the empty lot next to the hotel. That helped keep our minds off of the battle ahead of us. Some of the swimmers were young, like 15-year-old Bobby Hackett from New York City and 16-year-old Brian Goodell from Mission Viejo. But they got treated as and acted like veterans, not rookies.

We all believed strongly in the three coaches, Doc, George Haines (Santa Clara) and Don Gambril (Long Beach). Each one could have been the Head Coach. They worked really well together and shared equally in the coaching duties, almost as if we had three Head Coaches instead of one. They conditioned us well and built up our confidence. They made us believe that we could do better than the Sports Illustrated pre-Olympic predictions, which were that we would win about half of the men's swimming medals.

When we met that afternoon in the coaches' room of the Olympic Village on the first day of competition, we huddled together with our hands touching in the center. I was still walking on cloud nine, as I had been elected to carry the American flag in the Opening Ceremony the day before, leading the entire USA Olympic Team. It was the greatest honor of my life. As a team, we were confident that we would do well, but not as well as Doc was planning on. We looked down at our connected hands in the huddle, while Doc gave his final instructions.

"On three," he began, "let's shout the loudest *Let's Go!* you have ever heard. I want the women's Team to be able to hear us all the way down at their end of the Village."

"Oh, and by the way," he continued. "Tonight, we are going to start out by sweeping the men's 200 fly. And then, we are going to sweep every event after that."

Peering down at all our hands together, none of us really wanted to look up at Doc to see if he was really serious. Didn't he remember Pyttel held the World Record in the 200 butterfly? We were all thinking that getting two Americans on the podium would be great, but not Doc. He wanted it all.

On the count of three, we belted out the loudest *Let's Go!* that could possibly come from a couple of dozen vocal chords. Then we started to walk toward the door to make our way toward the Olympic Natatorium.

Before we could get out, though, Doc walked over to the closet in the corner of the small room and pulled out a broom and an American flag. He handed the broom to Jim Montgomery, our top sprinter and he handed the American flag to John Naber, one of our biggest stars.

"Jim and John," Doc continued. "I want you two to lead us over to the pool tonight. John, you just wave that big flag as high as you can. Jim, you just sweep that broom back and forth. While we are following behind you guys, we'll be chanting *Sweep, Sweep, Sweep!*

We walked together as a Team over to the Natatorium, John waving the flag and Jim sweeping the broom ahead of us. As we chanted *Sweep, Sweep, Sweep!* other athletes looked at us like we were a bit crazy. We didn't care. We just kept yelling out *Sweep, Sweep, Sweep!*

After taking our place in the Natatorium bleachers, the chant of *Sweep, Sweep, Sweep!* never faltered. Both the flag and the broom were being waved high over our heads. As the eight finalists marched around the pool to their starting block positions for the 200 butterfly, the chant continued, growing louder. The three American swimmers heard it clearly. They looked up at us, now standing on our feet, and smiled. They knew exactly what it meant. Pyttel, walking in front of the three Americans, also looked confident.

As the gun went off for the start, the East German wasted no time reminding everyone that he held the World Record. Pyttel and Forrester, who was in the outside lane, were out first at 50 meters. By the half way point, Bruner took over the lead with Forrester just behind him. Pyttel backed off the second fifty and turned almost even with Gregg.

On the third 50, Pyttel made his move, pulling ahead of all three swimmers, turning first at 150 meters. Forrester tried to stay with him. Pyttel came off the final turn into an almost all-out sprint, determined to get to the finish first. Forrester turned second, then Bruner, then Gregg. Now it was a fight to the finish. We kept yelling *Sweep, Sweep, Sweep!* We were all starting to feel as if that would not happen.

With 25 meters to go it was a dead lock between Pyttel, Gregg and Bruner. Any one of them could still win. Forrester seemed to be fading. We were now all on our feet screaming at the top our lungs *Sweep! Sweep! Sweep!*

With just 10 meters to the wall, Bruner and Gregg began to sprint to the wall. The East German was tying up. Bruner touched first for the gold with a World Record. Gregg finished second. Forrester put on a last second surge into the wall and somehow managed to get his hands on the wall for bronze, .06 seconds ahead of Pyttel. It was an American sweep.

The three American swimmers hugged each other, while we did the same in the stands. Steve Furniss was seated next to me. We looked at each other and I could tell we were both thinking the same thing.

"Doc was right. We swept the 200 butterfly. Maybe we *can* sweep every event in these Olympic Games. We can do this!"

For eight consecutive afternoons of the swimming competition, Doc and the other coaches called us into their room for another meeting. Each time, we would end on the loud *Let's Go!* cheer and Doc would hand the broom and the American flag to two new swimmers to lead us over to the finals. All along the way and inside the Natatorium we would chant *Sweep, Sweep, Sweep!* until the final race was swum on the final day.

By the time the week of swimming competition was over, we did not sweep every event. There were eleven individual swimming events in those Olympic Games and two relays. That means there were 33 individual swimming medals to be awarded to swimmers competing from 51 different countries. In total, the U.S. men won 25 of those 33 medals (76%), far more than the 16 medals Sports Illustrated had predicted we'd win. We left 8 medals; one gold, one silver and six bronze medals for the other 50 countries to take home. All the events, except one, were won in World Record times. Team USA won both men's swimming relays, also in World Record times. I was proudly part of one of the four American sweeps in the 100 meter butterfly, earning a bronze medal.

What was most remarkable to me was not that the American men dominated the swimming events, but by how much we dominated. One month earlier, each member of our Team had to swim his heart out just to qualify for the Olympic Team. There was no holding back at the Olympic

Trials. It was do or die. Yet nearly every single swimmer improved his time dramatically, often by seconds, not tenths, in the Olympic races just four weeks later. There is no physical or physiological explanation for what caused such a dramatic improvement in our performances.

There is a psychological explanation, however. It is called *team spirit*. Led by some great coaches using a chant, a flag and a broom, this unlikely group of swimmers united into an incredibly bonded American team. It was the *team spirit* of the 1976 men's US Olympic Swimming Team that resulted one of the most dominating athletic performances in Olympic history.

The Women's Story

While the men's team was razor-focused on its mission that week, the women's team got caught totally off guard. It was a strong US Women's Olympic swimming team, led by arguably the world's greatest female swimmer of the time, Shirley Babashoff. Shirley was world-class in every freestyle event from the 100 meters to the 800 meters and versatile enough to win the decathlon of swimming, the 400 meter individual medley. Including the two relays, Shirley was capable of winning six Olympic gold medals in Montreal. After her successful Olympic Trials, where she broke a World and several American records, Shirley had been hoisted onto a pedestal, being compared to the great Mark Spitz, who won seven gold medals in 1972.

Shirley could handle the expectations of the media and the pressure that comes along with it, even at the Olympic level. What she couldn't handle was the cheating. The East German women's Olympic team of Montreal was almost an entirely different squad than the one that had competed against the American women in a dual meet with Team USA in Concord, California in 1974.

The awareness and suspicion of East Germany systematically doping their female athletes, injecting them with anabolic steroids starting from before they had even reached puberty, began in 1973 in Belgrade, Yugoslavia. There, at the first World Championships, and just one year after a dismal showing in Munich at the 1972 Olympic Games, the East German women dominated the swimming competition. They won ten out of thirteen events on the schedule, all in World Record times.

At first, the humiliation in Belgrade and the new competition with East Germany served the American women well. They took the East German's miraculous improvements as nothing more than an extreme challenge, ignoring the truth that they then suspected. For the three years leading up to Montreal, our American women swimmers trained harder than ever before, vastly improving their times in every event to become more competitive with the East Germans.

By the time of the Olympic Trials of 1976, it looked as if our American women had leveled the playing field with East Germany. They were not going to face another embarrassment as they had in Belgrade. They were ready for battle, so they thought.

After arriving in Montreal, the women's team went to the Olympic Natatorium for the first time for a warm up swim. With the signs written in French, Shirley and a few of her teammates walked into the women's locker room and began to change into their training suits. Suddenly, some very deep voices could be heard coming from the row of lockers next to theirs. The US women quickly put their warmups back on and walked outside. Their first thought was that they had mistakenly entered the men's locker room. They hadn't.

What they heard were the voices of some of the East German women swimmers, masculinized from years of injections of male hormones. They were young women turned into men, bigger and stronger than normal, with hair on their faces.

On July 18, the same day the American men swept the 200 butterfly event, the East German women trounced the American women in the 400 medley relay, beating them by seven seconds. It wasn't even a race and was exemplary of what was to come.

On July 19, in the finals of the women's 100 meter freestyle, East Germany's Kornelia Ender won easily in World Record time, with her teammates placing 2nd and 6th. The three American women finished 4th, 5h and 7th, well behind the leaders. It was Shirley's first individual race and she placed 5th, though she was not expected to win.

She was expected to win the following day, however, in the finals of the 400 meter freestyle, an event she held the World Record. She placed second behind a virtually unknown East German swimmer, Petra Thumer. Both swimmers were under the previous World Record.

So it continued two days later, as Kornelia Ender defeated Shirley in the 200 freestyle for the gold medal, again in World Record time. By now, Shirley was getting demoralized. In the press conference after the 200 freestyle, she began to express her frustration and accused the East Germans of cheating. She was getting madder each day.

Surly Shirley is what the headlines read in the paper the following day. Now, she was not just a disappointment to the world, she was a sore loser. In an effort to save face and win at least one individual event, Shirley scratched from the 400 individual medley to concentrate on her other signature event, the 800 meter freestyle. It would be her last chance for an individual gold medal in these Olympic Games.

On July 25, on the final day of swimming competition, in a head-to-head race for 800 meters and in the final sprint to the finish, East German Petra Thumer out-touched Shirley by a few tenths of a second to win her second gold medal. Shirley finished with her fourth silver medal of the Olympic Games. Both swimmers were under the previous World Record. Shirley was mentally crushed.

Shirley and I swam on the same team in the summer, Huntington Beach Aquatic Club. From watching her beat me almost every day in practice, I knew how tough of a swimmer Shirley Babashoff was. I knew that if it came down to the last 10 meters of a race, no one could beat Shirley, at least not legally. She always somehow got her hand on the wall first. Until Montreal.

After finishing the 800 freestyle, her head hung down, staring at the water below. There she was, a beaten-down, dejected young woman 19 years of age, having given it her all, swimming her very best times faster than the previous World Records, but still not having a single gold medal to show for it. On top of that, the media thought she was a poor sport. The problem was that while she felt so mentally down, the American women still had one more event to go. It was the final event of the competition, the Women's 4 x 100 freestyle relay. Shirley was an important leg on that relay.

On paper, there was no way the American women could win the 4 x 100 freestyle relay. The three East German women that had swum in the finals of the 100 meter freestyle were over a half a second faster than the three American women in the same race. The winner, Kornelia Ender, was nearly a full second faster than her teammate in second place. The fourth swimmer on the American relay team, Wendy Boglioli, was really a butterflier, not a freestyler. She had never swum the 100 freestyle in under 57 seconds, which was slower than all of the other swimmers on both teams. It looked like the East German women were about to do the same thing that the US Men's team did, win every event in the Olympic swimming competition but one.

I don't really know exactly what happened that day after the women's 800 freestyle final and preceding the women's 400 free relay. I was sitting in the stands watching, feeling really sorry for Shirley. I was thinking that the last thing she probably wanted to do was to swim on a relay that had no chance of winning.

I understand that after Shirley warmed down from her 800 freestyle, the four women swimming on the relay got together before the final relay race. Then, with a couple of final words from Head Coach, Jack Nelson, who simply said, *"Make it happen"*, the four girls decided that they would. With the inspiration from the coaches, those four women decided that they were going to win the relay, cheats or no cheats. They were going to win the gold medal, no matter what it took. No one other than those girls and the coaches thought that could happen.

Kim Peyton, the fastest American woman, would lead off. Wendy Boglioli, the butterflier, would go second, a place traditionally held for the slowest member of the team. The third leg would be swum by 15-year-old Jill Sterkel, from California, who had placed 7th in the individual event. Shirley would swim the anchor leg and bring it home with whatever she had left in her. It didn't seem like there could be much left after the 800 meter swim and such an emotionally grueling week of competition.

As the teams paraded out to the starting blocks, the American women did not look defeated. They appeared dauntless and poised, like they were on a mission. They would be in Lane 3 right next to the fastest qualifying East German team in Lane 4; exactly where they wanted to be.

In a surprise move, East Germany decided to lead off their relay with their superstar, Kornelia Ender. They likely figured that they could get so far ahead, no one could catch them. Kim Peyton would just have to stay as close to her as she could. That is exactly what she did.

When the gun went off for the final relay race, both Kornelia and Kim swam nearly the exact times they had done in the individual 100 meter race. East Germany was now over a second ahead of the American women. From that point, East Germany expected to lengthen their lead, using their silver medalist and second fastest sprinter, Petra Priemer, for the next leg. The US butterflier from New Jersey, however, had another idea.

On her leg, Wendy Boglioli swam the most courageous swim of her life. She split 55.81 seconds, almost two seconds faster than she had ever swum the event before. Instead of lengthening their lead on the U.S. Team, the East Germans now found themselves in a battle with the Americans, just .7 seconds ahead of them.

The third leg of the relay turned out to be the most pivotal one. When Jill Sterkel jumped into the water, she looked like she was on a rampage to catch the East Germans. Imagine at barely 15 years of age having that kind of pressure, but Jill showed no fear. She simply swam out of her mind, catching the East German on the first 50 meters. Instead of fading on the second 50 meters, as we expected her to do, she passed the East German swimmer, Andrea Pollock. Her split of 55.78 was over a second faster than in her individual race and was the fastest split in the competition. Jill handed Shirley a slight lead going into the anchor leg by .4 seconds. Could Shirley hold on?

The physical and mental beating that Shirley had taken over the past week was extensive. She had just completed one of the most exhausting races on the schedule, only to get touched out at the end. Now, she was expected to pull off the miracle of miracles, beat the East German women. She was not about to get touched out one last time.

With incredible strength and fortitude, Shirley swam the anchor leg for the US Team in 56.32 seconds, holding off Claudia Hempel, who swam a lifetime best 56.56. It was a new World Record, but it was much more than that. It was retribution for what they knew East Germany had done. It was one of the most courageous demonstrations of mental toughness and resilience that I have ever seen in any sport.

When those four American girls huddled on the deck immediately after their victory, with their heads together and arms wrapped around each other's shoulders, the tears welled in my eyes. Finally, Shirley got her gold medal. It was *team spirit* that brought those four girls to an amazing achievement, against all odds.

The psychological trauma of what Shirley Babashoff went through that week took its toll on her. It effectively ended her swimming career. She became almost reclusive in life, never even attending a swimming event for decades. She worked (and still does) as a letter carrier for the US Postal Service in her home town of Fountain Valley, California.[3]

In 2016, at the 40-year anniversary of the 1976 Olympic swimming team, Shirley was honored for her successful career at the US Olympic Trials. After the Berlin Wall fell in 1989, documents were uncovered revealing the massive

---

[3] Shirley tells her entire story leading up to this epic battle with the East German swimmers and the media in her autobiography, *Making Waves,* with Chris Epting, Santa Monica Press 2016.

steroid doping scandal of the East Germans from that era. Many of the East German women athletes (not just swimmers) suffered extensive and irreparable damage from receiving such high doses of anabolic steroids for years, from the time they were children, leading to cancer, sterility, liver damage and many other medical problems. Of those athletes who could have children, some of them were born with birth defects, including blindness and club feet. The athletes were told they were being given injections of vitamins.[4]

Here is my best advice taken from this Olympic Team experience:

- **In life, whether you consider your family, your workplace, your school, your club or any other groups, you always will do better working as a team, rather than as an individual fending for yourself. Whatever teams you are on, put aside your self-interest. Get spirited. Like the U.S. Olympic swimmers of 1976, do what is best for the team. After all, life is a *team sport*, not an individual sport.**

---

[4] The events of this horrific tragedy are well documented in the film *The Last Gold*, released in 2016 and narrated by Emmy-award winner Julianna Margulies, and in the book, *Faust's Gold*, by Steven Ungerleider, PhD. St. Martin's Press 2001.

Lesson Five
Olympians never give up

"Never give up! Failure and rejection are only the first step to succeeding." – Jim Valvano

Of all the Olympic ideals, I would say that *perseverance* may be the most common trait of the Olympians. There is not one Olympian who has been successful in every single race or event. They all have fallen at some point in their career, and they have all learned to get back up and push on. Some have fallen more than others. None of them give up. Even more than Olympians, the Paralympians with significant physical disabilities have learned the true value of perseverance in life.

I have always had the greatest respect and admiration for the Olympians or Paralympians that have overcome the greatest challenges to become successful. One of my favorite Olympic stories about perseverance is of a swimmer that you have probably never heard of. His name is Michael Burton, who won three individual gold medals in the 1968 and 1972 Olympic Games. On my list of the all-time top-ten mentally-toughest swimmers, Mike Burton is number two, just behind Michael Phelps.[5] Mike Burton did

---

[5] In my opinion, Michael Phelps deserves to be first on the *mental toughness* list not for having won 28 Olympic medals, but for having won one of them (200 meter butterfly in Beijing 2008) with his goggles filled with water. He also impressed me in 2012 in London after swimming poorly on the first day of competition (400 IM), yet he came back after that poor showing to swim very well in his other Olympic events.

not have the swimming talent of Michael Phelps, but he had the heart of a lion and the eye and tenacity of a tiger.

When he was nine years old, living in Sacramento, California, Mike Burton fell off of his bicycle and broke his leg. Mike was an active child, so having a cast on his leg for a few months nearly killed his spirit. When the cast came off and the doctor told him he couldn't run for a few more months, he became even more despondent.

"What can I do?" Mike asked the doctor.

"You can swim", he replied.

Mike Burton's swimming career started that day, and, just like Forrest Gump ran in the movie, Mike swam and he swam.

He was not blessed with great swimming talent. He grew to be 5 feet 9 inches tall, short for most elite swimmers. He didn't have big hands nor have big feet, either. But he could outwork anyone in the pool.

Under the coaching of Sherm Chavoor, one of America's greatest swimming coaches, Mike worked his way up the ladder to become the best distance freestyler in America. Eventually, he became the best in the world.

After finishing his college swimming career at UCLA, where he won several individual NCAA Championship races, he prepared himself well, working extra hard for what he thought would be his final swimming competition, the 1968 Olympic Games of Mexico City.

The high altitude of Mexico City was not kind to the distance athletes of any sport. Jim Ryun, the greatest distance 1500 meter runner of his day, was defeated soundly in his specialty race at the Olympic Games by Kip Keino from Kenya, who had trained his entire life at altitude.

In Mexico City, Mike Burton would swim the 400 meter and 1500 meter freestyle events, which is the equivalent in track and field to running the 1500 meters and the 5000 meter events. Mike didn't have a lifetime to prepare for the altitude, just six weeks of training in Colorado Springs before the Olympic Games began.

In both races, Mike's competitive tenacity and mental toughness were apparent. Even in the rarified air of 7,000 feet above sea level, he demolished his competition, winning the Olympic gold medals in both races by large margins.

It seemed to be a fitting end to a storybook swimming career for Mike Burton. In those days, there was really no opportunity for a swimmer to compete at an elite level after college. For Mike, the Olympic Games of Mexico City came at an ideal time. Winning two gold medals there was a perfect way to end his career. But he wasn't quite finished, yet.

In the four years after Mexico City, as the 1972 Olympic Games of Munich drew nearer, there was a new king of distance freestyle swimming. His name was Rick DeMont. Unlike the aggressive, attacking fast strokes of Burton, Rick DeMont's freestyle was as beautiful and graceful as anyone had ever seen. Fueled by a powerful kick, the young 16-year-old DeMont was a rising superstar, setting World Records and coming into his prime just in time for Munich. The World Records in the 400 meter and 1500 meter freestyle events were much faster than Mike Burton had ever swum.

Undeterred by the new standard of fast distance swimming, Mike Burton decided some time in 1971, three years into his retirement, that he still had some great swims left in him. He headed back to the pool with Shavoor and started to make his comeback to try for another Olympic Team.

The 1972 Olympic Trials were held in Portage Park, Illinois, a suburb of Chicago on August 2-6. One of the first events on the schedule was the men's 400 meter freestyle. Burton failed to make the finals. Not surprisingly, Rick DeMont won the event. Burton had only one more chance to qualify for the Olympic Team and that was in the 1500 meter freestyle on the last day of competition.

Mike was the eighth and final qualifier for the event, sneaking into the finals by just tenths of seconds ahead of the 9th place finisher. In the finals, swimming in the outside lane, Mike set a torrid pace, leading the field at 100 meters by a full body length. It was the only race strategy he knew -- go out fast and hold on.

By 800 meters, two other Americans, DeMont and Doug Northway, had already caught and passed him. Now the battle was to see who would earn the third spot on the Team. For the remaining 700 meters of the race, three American swimmers were neck and neck trying to get that coveted third place.

DeMont won the race in a new World Record time. Northway finished second. Somehow, Burton miraculously found the strength on the final 50 meters to sprint home and touch ahead of the other two Americans. The crowd went wild, offering a standing ovation for the Old King of Distance Swimming, Burton, and the newly-crowned freestyle King, DeMont. Mike Burton was on the Olympic Team again.

The training camp for the Men's Olympic Swimming Team was held at West Point, New York, where we made our final preparations for Munich. Unlike Mexico City, the conditions of Munich would be ideal for every athlete to perform well. The Germans built new state of the art facilities for every sporting venue. On a trip to Russia in 1971 as part of the USA National Team, we stopped in Munich to see the construction of the pool. It was meant to inspire us and it did.

During the training camp, I observed Mike Burton doing what he did best, outworking everyone. Several times, he stayed after practice to do extra sets to get himself ready. DeMont and Northway, the other two Americans in the 1500 meter race, did not seem overly concerned about Burton. At 25 years of age, he was considered too old to be much of a threat to them.

The structure of the Olympic Natatorium, similar to the Olympic Stadium, was tent-like, with tall massive steel beams supporting a vast translucent plastic roof cascading to all sides from its pinnacle. From afar, with all of its banners and surrounding flags waving in the wind, the Natatorium and Olympic Stadium appeared to be a like an enormous modern circus. Yet, once inside, there was no doubt of its permanence or beauty. 10,000 empty seats overlooked the aqua blue color of the crystal-clear water contrasted against the bright yellow lane markers. The Olympic pool simply invited swimmers to swim fast.

On the first day of competition, that is precisely what Rick DeMont did by winning the 400 meter freestyle in World Record time, just ahead of the Australian swimmer, Brad Cooper. The young 16-year-old phenom showed no sign of fear nor intimidation. Mark Spitz, my roommate at the 1972 Olympic Games, began his quest to win seven gold medals by winning the 200 meter butterfly. I finished well behind him in second place. Robin Backhaus, another American, finished third for a clean sweep. It was an incredibly strong start for the American men.

Unfortunately, the momentum did not continue. On the morning of the second day, our coaches received a call from the International Olympic Committee informing them that Rick DeMont had been disqualified in the 400 meter freestyle. He failed the drug test. Not only did he have to return his gold medal, he would later discover that he was disqualified from competing in his other event, the 1500 meter freestyle. In effect, the disqualification would cost Rick two Olympic gold medals.[6]

---

[6] In 2001 the USOC admitted that it had mishandled DeMont's medical information at the 1972 Olympics and appealed to the IOC to reinstate the medal. To date, the IOC has not officially changed the race results nor overturned his ban. Rick DeMont has never given up in his quest to get his gold medal back.

His drug test was positive for ephedrine, a banned substance. Ephedrine was an ingredient in the asthma medicine that Rick had inhaled prior to every race, ever since he was a young age group swimmer in Marin County, California, and was diagnosed with asthma. A few times in the past, when he had failed to use the medicine before a race, he was stricken with such severe bronchial constriction, induced by the exercise, the attack led him to stop swimming or slow down and rest on the wall. Rick could not afford to have that happen during the most important race of his life in the Olympic Games. He did what he always did before racing and took a puff from the inhaler.

If you are wondering why Rick was not warned about the use of the medicine in the Olympic Games, so was he. In fact, I sat next to Rick during our Olympic physical exam after qualifying for the team. He wrote an extensive list of his allergies and medications, including drugs and foods. Not once was he asked about his asthma, nor his asthma medication, by the USOC medical team. Not once did anyone look through his DOP kit to see what medicine he might have in there. Rick was totally in the dark and unwarned.

Regardless of the mishap and how it happened, Rick was not told until the morning of the preliminary 1500 meter race, three days after the failed drug test and while waiting in the *Ready Room*, that he would not be allowed to compete in that event. There were just two Americans left, Northway and Burton. In the preliminary heats of the 1500 meter freestyle, an Australian, Graham Windeatt qualified first, the only swimmer under 16 minutes. Burton qualified second, nearly ten seconds behind Windeatt, and Northway qualified fourth for the final. The other Australian, Brad Cooper, who was awarded the gold medal in the 400 meters after the DeMont disqualification, qualified third.

Like the men's marathon in track and field, the men's 1500 meter freestyle is always contested on the final day of competition. The American swimmers who were not competing sat up in the stands, very excited about the events to come on the final night of competition. Outside of the Natatorium, crowds of hundreds of people gathered 10 to 20 deep all the way around the building. They were less interested in watching the 1500 meter freestyle than they were hoping to catch a glimpse of Mark Spitz winning his seventh gold medal on the final event, the 400 meter medley relay. They wanted to see history being made, which was about to happen.

The first event, however, was the men's 1500 meter freestyle and history was about to be made in this event, also. As the men were paraded up to the blocks, Burton had that look of the tiger in his eyes. He knew that this would be the last race of his competitive career. He wanted to make the best of it.

The start of the men's 1500 race was no surprise to anyone. Burton went out fast, as he always did and was almost a body length ahead of the field. However, just as happened in Portage Park at the Olympic Trials, by 800 meters, Windeatt caught and passed Burton. Cooper, the other Australian, looked like he was about to do the same thing.

When Windeatt took over the lead, the entire Australian swimming team stood up and cheered loudly, looking over at us sitting next to them. There was no love between the American and Australian swimmers. They knew then that they had the gold medal won and were rubbing it in our faces. They knew Burton's history and thought he was finished. The only question in their mind was would Windeatt break the World Record and could they also get the silver medal?

Our thought at this moment was whether Mike could hold on for a medal, or could Northway come back strong and possibly sneak in for a medal? Since none of us were expecting Burton to win, getting any medal would be an amazing accomplishment in his comeback effort. Swimming is not like a distance race in track, where the lead often changes hands throughout the race. Once a swimmer is overtaken, he or she almost never is able to come back and retake the lead. Almost never.

Mike Burton was no ordinary swimmer. By the time the swimmers had reached 1000 meters in the race, it became apparent to all of us that Mike was beginning to shorten the gap between himself and Windeatt. Cooper was fading back, and Northway was coming on strong as we expected.

At the turn at 1,200 meters, Burton had succeeded in catching Windeatt. When he made the turn, the entire US team got on its feet and started screaming loudly. We looked over at the Australian team, now seated and quiet. Their celebration had been premature.

For the final 300 meters, Mike continued to pour it on, extending his lead by 8 meters. He won the Olympic gold medal in his final race in World Record time, finishing almost six seconds ahead of Windeatt. Northway finished third. It was one of the most heroic swims I had ever seen.

Later that evening, Mike invited me to celebrate with him at the famous Hofbrau Haus in downtown Munich. While we celebrated his victory, with him proudly wearing his gold medal, I stared in awe at him. Spitz's record of seven gold medals and seven World Records in one Olympic Games was incredible. Not to diminish his accomplishment, I knew Mark was capable of doing that.

However, in all my life, I had never seen anyone pull off a comeback in either a career or a race, as Mike had done. I didn't expect it. To me, his 1500 meter victory was the most impressive swim of the Olympic Games. Finally, I had to ask him.

"Mike," I asked. "How did you do that?"

He looked at me like I had just asked a really dumb question.

"What do you mean?" he responded.

"How did you pull that off? In all of my life, I have never seen anyone get overtaken like you did, yet have the strength to come back and win. Where did that second wind come from?"

"Gary," he answered. "In all of my life, I have never, ever given up in a race. I was not about to start tonight."

His answer gave me goosebumps.

To become Olympians, athletes falter, struggle, lose occasionally. Sometimes they get discouraged. They just never give up. Learn from them.

- **In life, whatever your quest, it won't come easily. Remember the most important Olympic ideal, *perseverance,* and never give up. It is the only way that you will reach your goal.**

Lesson Six
The World should be one big Olympic Village

"A fundamental concern for others in our individual and community lives would go a long way in making the world the better place we so passionately dreamt of." – Nelson Mandela

After celebrating Mike Burton's victory at the conclusion of the Olympic swimming events, I decided to stay the night at the Bayerischer Hof Hotel in downtown Munich. The small cots we were using to sleep on in the Olympic Village were neither comfortable nor conducive to a good night's sleep. After so much stress and excitement, I badly needed sleep.

One day after the Olympic competition ended, our swimming governing body made a promise to the German Swimming Federation to take the entire Team to Regensburg, about 50 miles from Munich, to swim in an exhibition. The bus was scheduled to leave the Olympic Village at noon. The trip was not optional. We were so exhausted, no one on our Team really wanted to go.

Reluctantly, I set my alarm at the hotel early enough on Tuesday, September 5 to allow enough time to take the U-Bahn back to the Olympic Village and catch the team bus to Regensburg. As I jumped off of the subway, destined for the Village and ran up the escalator onto the street, I began to notice that things were different.

There were normally many people walking around the outskirts of the Village on the sidewalks, but now there were sirens and police cars everywhere. People and vehicles all seemed to be heading toward the Village. I glanced down at one of the newspapers displayed at a kiosk, as I stepped up my pace, quickly interpreting the headlines. I understood enough German to read the word *killed* in one of them. My curiosity was building. Something bad had happened. I just didn't know what.

By the time I reached the entrance to the Olympic Village, there must have been 200 people in front of me all trying to get in. In either direction, all I could see were people lined up around the chain-linked fence surrounding the Village in both directions, many of them hoisting cameras into the air to take photos. Police car after police car, blue lights swirling and sirens blasting loudly, lined the streets behind them.

I pushed and shoved my way all the way up to the front of the crowd, fearing I would miss the bus leaving for Regensburg. When I finally arrived at the guard post, I reached into my pocket to take out my ID and credentials. It was empty.

"Shit", I thought to myself. "I left my ID in my hotel room".

I was not going to talk my way in. Not today.

For the next 30 minutes I peered through the guard gate into the Village, noting that very few people were walking about. Unless I could spot a friend, I knew I would not be able to get in. Finally, I saw George Haines, one of our coaches, walking by.

"George!!" I screamed at the top of my voice, whistling loudly after my scream. He heard me and came toward me. He looked pale, very despondent.

"George, what happened?" I asked, still completely unaware of the terrorist attack.

"It's over" he answered, solemnly.

"What do you mean, *it's over*?" I asked.

"The Olympic Games are over. Some terrorists got into the Village last night and killed a bunch of Israeli athletes. In fact, the terrorists are still in there right now with some hostages." He pointed up to one of the Village apartment buildings very near where we were standing. "This is the end of the Olympic Games. It's over".

I felt a sickness in my stomach. How could this have happened? How could the Olympic Games, standing for world peace, be marred by this terrorist attack. I couldn't believe that it happened. No one could.

It took about an hour longer for George to return with some new credentials to get me into the Village. Inside, what was normally a beehive of activity, with athletes and coaches coming and going in all directions, suddenly was a ghost town. It was spooky, eerily quiet.

When I got back to my room in the USA building, I was met by two strange men standing outside the door. I walked into my room to find a few of my teammates seated outside on the balcony, staring across the courtyard at the building where the Israeli athletes were being held hostage. My roommate, Mark Spitz, was not there. The concrete floor was covered with unopened congratulatory Western Union telegrams littered on the floor. There was a cafeteria tray with half a meal left on it sitting on the table.

"Where is Mark?" I asked. "And who are those men outside?"

"Mark is gone" answered John Murphy, another Indiana swimmer. "We don't know where they took him. They didn't say. They just left with him in a hurry. Oh, and those two guys are FBI agents."[7]

I looked across the courtyard at the Israeli building, located just 500 yards from where we were seated. We all felt sick and helpless. There was no sign of life or of movement.

The exhibition trip to Regensburg was not cancelled. In fact, we preferred to get out of the Village. By the time we returned to the Village late that evening, the Palestinian terrorists and the Israeli hostages remaining were still holed up in their room. Not much had changed. The Palestinian demand to release 234 prisoners jailed in Israel had not been

---

[7] Being Jewish, Mark Spitz was considered a possible target of the Palestinian terrorists. He was disguised early that morning, put into the trunk of a Mercedes Benz and taken to the airport. From there he flew to London to safety.

met. Two of the Israeli athletes were dead inside their apartments in the Village.

At around 10 p.m. that night the eight Palestinian terrorists, called *Black September,* planned to escape with the 9 remaining Israeli hostages to Furstenfeldbruck Air Field via helicopter, where they would board a Boeing 727 to take them back to Palestine.

The German crisis team posted snipers at the airport and had policemen dressed as flight attendants on board the aircraft. At around 11 p.m. the German marksmen opened fire on the terrorists as they were leaving their helicopters. The visibility was not ideal and some of the terrorists were not struck with the gunfire. One that was not hit unleashed a hand grenade into the helicopter holding all nine remaining Israelis. Instantly, they tragically perished in the explosion. Three of the eight terrorists were taken alive.

After a single day of mourning for the Israeli athletes and coaches who died in the attack held at Olympic Stadium, the IOC elected to continue on with the Olympic Games as planned. It was not the same and never will be again. The terrorist attack in Munich changed the Olympic Games forever, much as 9/11 did for the rest of the world.

Before Munich, security costs for the Olympic Games were measured in the tens of thousands of dollars. Today, security costs during the Olympic Games are in the tens of billions of dollars. The projected bill for the Tokyo Olympic Games is expected to reach $15 billion. Even so, the threat of another terrorist attack during the Olympic Games always looms.

Before Munich, the Olympic Village was supposed to represent a microcosm of the ideal world. It was part of De Coubertin's dream of world peace. I was in Mexico City and Munich, before Black September, so I remember what it was like. The Olympic Village was a small world of around 10,000 people of all sizes and shapes, colors and religions, cultures and habits, living peacefully together for just over two weeks. It was a safe place where athletes mingled, traded pins, shared stories, and took pictures together. People respected each other as fellow athletes. Everyone, or so it seemed, got along with one another.

In Mexico City in 1968, as a young 17-year-old swimmer, the Olympic Games was so new to me, the first international meet I had ever been in, I didn't know what to think. It was like pitching your first Major League game in the World Series. I was just taking it all in, fascinated by the hype and the sheer number of different athletes, coming in all shapes and sizes.

One day, while walking back from the dining room in the Olympic Village, I was so awestruck, I managed to walk into the wrong building housing the athletes. The nine-story building housing the Team USA athletes looked identical to the one next to it, housing the athletes from the USSR. Oblivious to my mistake, I walked directly into the empty elevator and pushed the button for the ninth floor.

Before the doors had a chance to close, into the elevator walked this giant of man, wearing sky blue warmups with the letters CCCP emblazoned on the front. He took up nearly the entire elevator, as I quietly squeezed myself into the back corner. He was breathing heavily, sweat beading out on his forehead. His chest was so large that his arms hung down at an angle of about 30 degrees from his body, unlike the arms that would hang straight down in normal-sized human beings. His deep-set, penetrating eyes stared down at me like two laser beams, examining the USA that was written on my warm up top. Suddenly, the doors closed.

"Oh my God," I thought to myself. "Did I just enter the wrong building?"

If the size of this man, whom I now recognized as Leonid Zhabotinsky, the Super Heavyweight Soviet weightlifter, the strongest man in the world, was not enough to make me shake, the stench from his soiled warmups was.

I looked up at the lights going on the floors as we steadily climbed upward, occasionally glancing up at the face of the giant. His breathing became louder. He couldn't take his eyes off of the USA written on my warmups. It seemed like the slowest elevator on earth. My palms were sweating.

Finally, we reached the seventh floor and the doors opened. He turned to walk out, but before leaving, he quickly turned back and in his deep voice, blurted out this song.

"*My baby duz ze hanky panky…my baby duz ze hanky panky.*" It was his Soviet rendition of the hit pop song from Tommy James and the Shondells.

I broke out laughing. I just realized that the Soviet athletes were not really that much different than the American athletes.

The terrorism of Munich changed the Olympic Village and the Olympic Games forever. Wouldn't it be nice if we could someday go back to the Olympic Village that is not secured like a prison? Where we could walk into the wrong elevator and still be alright? Wouldn't it be nice if we could go back to airports the way they used to function, without long security lines?

Sadly, those things will never happen. The world has changed. It has never been a safe place for everyone, and likely never will be. The Olympic Games and the Olympic Village are no longer as safe as we once thought. They likely never will be.

That does not mean you shouldn't strive for world peace. You should. Let us never forget that at one time, the Olympic Village, with all of its diverse human beings, was a great example of how the world can live together peacefully, even if for a few weeks. Perhaps the people of the world can co-exist as they once did in the Olympic Village. Anything is possible.

- **Striving for peace in the world is not simply something that you should do. To help maintain any semblance of global peace and harmony, it is essential that you keep trying. We must all strive for peace.**

Lesson Seven
Life always offers a Do-over

"For what it's worth, it's never too late to be whoever you want to be. I hope you live a life you're proud of, and, if you find that you're not, I hope you have the strength to start over." – F. Scott Fitzgerald

As a young boy growing up in California, I spent many hours playing stick ball, or kick ball or softball at the neighborhood playground. There is a lot of hand-eye coordination involved in those sports. Since I was just learning those skills, I often struck out or missed the ball completely in an attempt to knock it with my bat or stick or foot. On such occasions, frustrated by my failure, I would often ask for a *do-over*. It was one more chance to hit the ball and redeem myself. I wasn't as bad as I looked. Since my friends often found themselves in the very same position, it was customary to grant the request for a *do-over*.

In the Olympic Games, there are some sports or events that offer a *do-over*. In track and field, for example, an athlete doesn't just get one try in the long jump, high jump, pole vault, javelin, discus or shot put, for example. Each athlete gets three attempts, two *do-overs*, just in case the first one did not go as planned.

Other sports do not offer a *do-over*. On the final dive of the competition, if the diver overreaches or misses the entry, he or she doesn't get another chance to try it again. In the finals of the swimming competition or in the 100 meter dash in track, if the athlete has a bad start or turn, there is no second chance.

In Mexico City at the 1968 Olympic Games, Micki King was well on her way to winning the gold medal in the finals of the 3-meter springboard diving competition. On her second to last dive, she misjudged her twist and struck her arm against the diving board, fracturing her arm in the process. She managed to somehow still complete the dive, but earned very low scores on it. She wished she could do that one over again. Unbelievably, she completed her final dive, the most challenging one on her schedule, with a broken arm and in excruciating pain. Her score was not enough to win the gold medal. There was no *do-over*.[8]

On the final day of the Olympic Swimming Trials of 1972, in Portage Park, Illinois, I walked into the locker room to change clothes. I was feeling pretty good, after making the Olympic Team in three events, the 200 meter butterfly and both individual medley events, the 200 meter and 400 meter. In the latter two, I had set new World Records.

Sitting on the bench next to the locker was a friend of mine from Southern California, Frank Heckl. His face was buried in his hands and he was sobbing, almost uncontrollably. One year before, Frank had won 7 gold medals in the Pan American Games. He was the world's fastest swimmer that year. But this was 1972, the year of the

---

[8] Micki King came back in the 1972 Olympic Games and won her gold medal in the same event. In a way, her *do-over* occurred four years later.

Olympic Games. His lifelong dream was to qualify for an Olympic Team, yet he failed in his final attempt.[9]

To get to the Olympic Games in swimming, there is only one meet that counts, the Olympic Trials. It is called the *Meet from Heaven or Hell*, because you either make the Team, or you don't. Not many do. For Frank and so many others, there was no second chance; no *do-over*.

On the morning of August 30, 1972, I awoke feeling tired. I had tossed and turned the entire night on the small army cot in our room in the Olympic Village in Munich. I barely slept. Even with a full day to recover after winning the silver medal in the 200 meter butterfly, I did not feel ready for this day. I was thinking all night about today's race.

Today was the day of the 400 meter individual medley (IM), my best event. It was an event in which I held the World Record and hadn't lost since I won the silver medal in Mexico City four years earlier. My World Record was seven seconds faster than the second fastest swimmer in the world at that time. If anyone could claim *ownership* of the 400 IM, it was me. I had waited four years for this day, a chance to win the Olympic gold medal.

When I went to the pool to warm up for the preliminaries, I didn't feel particularly good. Nonetheless, I didn't need to be 100%. I could qualify easily for the finals later that evening, go back to the Village, eat, take a nap and be ready for the finals. All I needed to do was qualify.

---

[9] Dr. Frank Heckl, perhaps hungrier from not making an Olympic Team, went on to become a very successful Orthopedic Surgeon in Albuquerque, New Mexico.

In my preliminary heat, I swam against a Swedish swimmer, Bengt Gingsjo. He attended USC and I had swum against him many times. I knew I was much better than him. For 300 meters, we stayed almost even. On the final 100 meter freestyle leg, I recall trying to pick up the pace, just to prove that I could swim faster whenever I wanted to, and certainly faster than Bengt. There was nothing there; no energy. Instead, Bengt pulled ahead of me and beat me in the heat. I never felt helpless like that before in this event. I recall the first thought that popped into my head.

"Oh my God. I am going to lose this race tonight". That was the worst thing I could have done.

The rest of that day was a nightmare. It was the longest day of my life. I was scared, nervous, panicky. My resting pulse never went below 100. I couldn't eat without getting sick. I couldn't sleep.

My girlfriend at the time, Mary, came to the Village to see me. I was nearly as white as the sheets I lay on. She could see the panicked look on my face. Immediately, she ran to the cafeteria and brought back a juicy steak and potatoes from the dining room. The food in the Village in Munich was exceptionally good. I took one look at it and thought I would vomit. I couldn't get one bite down.

Mary went to my coach, Doc Counsilman, pleading for help. Doc came to visit me and even after he cracked a few of his stupid jokes, I smiled but couldn't relax. I was self-destructing - choking in front of their eyes. Nobody seemed capable of pulling me out of the tailspin.

I never was able to eat anything before the finals that same evening, nor rest. I stood up on the block in Lane 6, fourth qualifier for the finals, still nervous, but resolved to do the best I could. I was worried about what that might be. Like a rabbit running away from the foxes, I went out way too fast in the first two legs, butterfly and backstroke. By the time I turned for the breaststroke, my legs were dead. By the end of the breaststroke, three swimmers had passed me. It was all I could do to just to finish the race, finishing fifth.

Another American, Tim McKee, swam his best time by seconds and tied the Swede, Gunnar Larsson, to the hundredth of a second in 4:31.98, over a second slower than my World Record from the Trials. The timing system showed that Larsson had won by 2/1000 of a second, less than the margin of error of the timing equipment. Yet Larsson was given the gold medal and McKee the silver medal. It was not a fair decision. They should have both shared the gold medal.

I felt as if my world had collapsed. I felt as if I had let America down, my coaches down, and myself down. I had not represented my country well. I was dejected. I walked outside the Natatorium, sat down during the medal ceremony for the 400 IM and cried.

After a day or two of moping, I did manage to return to my normal self and finished the last two events on my Olympic schedule well. I swam my best time in the 200 IM, almost a full second under the previous World Record. Unfortunately, three other swimmers swam even faster, so I finished fourth. Unlike the 400 IM, I did the best I could.

I was o.k. with not winning. On the final day, I helped the American relay qualify in the preliminaries for the gold medal in the 400 medley relay by swimming the butterfly leg with my best time ever.

For the Olympic gold in the 400 IM, however, there was no *do-over.*

When it comes to second chances, life is not quite as harsh as some of the Olympic events. Sometimes in life, you don't quite get it right the first time. You need that second chance or *do-over.*

It may be with any of the five events of life's pentathlon that you need that second chance. Whether it is with your faith, your family, your profession, your community or your health, you will almost always get a *do-over*, a chance to make it right. Often, it turns out to be the best thing you ever did.

When I was essentially forced out of medicine in 2006, I needed a *do-over.* Even at 55, I felt young enough to start over doing something. I moved to the Florida Keys to start a new chapter in my life with a new profession.

My son, Gary Jr, founded The Race Club in 2003 in the Florida Keys to help aspiring Olympic swimmers reach their goals. By the time he retired in 2008, The Race Club needed a swimming coach, so I started coaching. Gary Jr gave me the opportunity for a *do-over*, for which I was very grateful. He helped breathe new life into an older body.

The Olympic Games does not always offer a *do-over,* but life often does.

- A *do-over* does not always mean starting over. Sometimes, it just means taking a new approach in life to improve your pentathlon scores in your weaker events. Either way, life is pretty generous and understanding when it comes to *do-overs.* It is never too late for you to start.

Lesson Eight
Gold Medalists are brave

"I'm definitely not a fearless individual but I am lucky that whatever fear I have inside me, my desire to win is always stronger." - Serena Williams

At The Race Club, we run camps for swimmers on how to improve their swimming technique. We also try to teach them how to be better people.

On the final day of our Race Club camps, we discuss mental toughness, one of the most common traits of the Olympians. Recently, my oldest son, Gary Jr, who won 10 Olympic swimming medals in 10 Olympic races, assisted me with one of our camps. When he spoke about mental toughness, he concluded with this thought:

"When you stand up on the starting block at your Championship meet, you must be brave."

I had seldom heard the word *brave or bravery* used in the context of sports, but it is true. To excel in the heat of major competition, athletes need to be brave. They cannot succeed with fear or doubt. The following story attests to Gary's bravery as an athlete.

On the afternoon of January 6, 1993, the six children of Charles Keating Jr, their husbands or wives, including my wife and I, and 21 grandchildren crammed into our bedroom with his wife, Mary Elaine. Even with the air conditioning going full blast, the room was extremely warm from the nervous body heat of so many anxious, tense humans packed closely together in one room. As we watched the television screen in front of us of the final day of the live coverage of Mr. Keating's trial in Los Angeles, we held each other's hands tightly. The tension from what was about to occur was unnerving, almost unbearable.

Outside our Paradise Valley home in Arizona, parked in the few shaded spots in the shade under the Palo Verde trees were FBI agents, the same ones that had been there nearly every day for the past two years. They were the agents that worked for Special FBI Agent James Whalen, who was brought in to Phoenix to direct the Keating investigation and ultimately, to imprison Charles Keating.

To that end, the agents sitting outside our home listened attentively with their audio technology directed toward the house, hoping to catch a conversation that might lead them to another indictment or, if they were lucky, perhaps to the discovery of the alleged millions of dollars from Lincoln Savings and Loan that they believed had been stolen.

For the previous two years, while on their way to school, our children passed these FBI agents sitting in their cars on the street, knowing exactly who they were and what they were up to. In fact, Gary Jr, the oldest Keating grandchild, went to high school and swam on the same team with Agent Whalen's son, Chris. To say that Gary and Chris did not get along would be a gross understatement. The swimming coach kept the two of them separated in workouts at all times.

Rather than fly out to Los Angeles for the jury's verdict and become a party to what had become a veritable media circus during the trial, the extended Keating family chose to remain at home and watch the outcome of the trial on television. It was hard not being there for someone we all loved, but we felt it was better this way. Most of us in the room, especially the adults, had a sick feeling about what was going to happen. Throughout the entire trial, we had watched the prosecutors portray Mr. Keating as a greedy, self-serving CEO who lived a lavish lifestyle, plundering from the S & L and stealing from the elderly.

Charlie Keating was the scapegoat for the S & L debacle of the 1980's.[10] Over 275 front-page articles in two years branded him as the official *villain* of the Savings and Loan crisis. According to Paul Craig Roberts, Chairman of the Institute for Political Economy in Washington D.C., and Lawrence M. Stratton, Robert Krieble Fellow at the Institute for Political Economy and former adjunct professor of Law at Georgetown University Law Center:

Charles Keating was the victim of an ancient injustice-a bill of attainder. He was convicted of a crime that did not exist until he was charged with it. The crime was not on the statute books but was pieced together by prosecutors from civil offenses and converted into a felony.[11]

---

[10] Barth J. R., Trimbath S., Yago G., *The Savings and Loan Crisis:* Lessons from a Regulatory Failure; 143-178. Kluwer Academic Publishers. The Milken Institute Series on Financial Innovation and Economic Growth. 2004.
[11] Roberts P. C. and Stratton L. M., *The Tyranny of Good Intentions: How Prosecutors and Law Enforcement Are Trampling the Constitution in the Name of Justice.* 50-54. Three Rivers Press 2008.

Whether he really was or wasn't the bad guy the media described no longer mattered. To the public, the perception that he was the symbol of greed had become the reality. Fake news or not, the government needed a villain and they found one in Charlie Keating, even though there was little real evidence of such. The FBI was simply brought in to deliver the final blow.

Even a continuous prayer of *Hail Mary, full of Grace* recited loudly by nearly everyone in the room, surrounded by the Crucifixes and Catholic relics, did not seem to ease the tension. We stood in front of the television watching nervously as the jury reconvened inside the crowded Los Angeles Courtroom. Judge Lance Ito, the same one who presided over and mishandled the O.J. Simpson trial, turned to the summoned jury.

"Has the jury reached a verdict?" he asked.

"We have, your Honor," responded the lead juror.

"And what is your verdict?" Judge Ito asked.

"Guilty on 73 counts of racketeering, fraud and conspiracy".

Inside our bedroom, the family prayer suddenly turned into wailing cries. The verdict and the imprisonment of Charlie Keating that would follow would change our lives forever. For a moment, I gazed around the room, observing the tears streaming down the faces of everyone there, except one person, Gary Jr.

His grandfather stood in the courtroom stoically, emotionless, staring straight-ahead, while the cameras panned in for a close up view of his face, hoping to see him break down. Instead, what the world saw was a man of strength and conviction, a virtual non-reaction to the verdict. Gary Jr stood the same way, emotionless in the back of the bedroom. Like his grandfather, the single person Gary idolized, he would not allow the media nor the biased jury to break him. At sixteen years of age, Gary would be as strong as his grandfather.

Before Charlie Keating reported to the Tucson Federal Penitentiary later that year, where he would remain for four and a half years until his convictions were overturned, he had a chance to watch Gary Jr swim in his high school Championship meet. Inspired by his grandfather being in the crowd, Gary lowered his time for the 100-yard freestyle in the finals by 4 seconds, and narrowly missed winning the race. The swimmer who beat Gary was much bigger and stronger than him, but that did not matter. He was not afraid. It was on that day that I first realized how brave Gary was as an athlete.

Charles Keating was not perfect, not by a long shot. He was also not the villain that the media and prosecutors portrayed him to be. In life, there are people who never dream nor dare to be great. They just coast through life, usually taking more than giving. Then, there are those who dream, but never do anything about making the dream happen. There are those who dream and try to make the dream happen, but don't know how, or fail to do so. Finally, there are those people who dream big and make the dream happen. It is a rare bunch. Charlie Keating was one of those people. He was a doer.

It was rarely mentioned by the media that Charles Keating was a successful businessman, long before he purchased Lincoln Savings and Loan. Working as Executive Vice President of American Financial Corporation in Cincinnati, he learned much from one of America's most successful businessmen, Carl Lindner. Charlie was the lead negotiator in some of Lindner's most important deals, such as the purchase of National General Corporation, which held Great American Insurance Company, a prized asset, and the Cincinnati *Enquirer*, that even Warren Buffett was unable to purchase. In Arizona, Keating turned the homebuilding company, Continental Homes, into one of the nation's leading builders.

However, the greatest testimony to the character of Charlie Keating is not his successful business deals, but what transpired while he was imprisoned. He was not sent to some white-collar criminal prison, but rather, by design, to a high-security federal prison, heavily populated by some tough gangs of mostly Hispanic and African Americans. There was even a tight group of Irish prisoners there from the IRA that no one messed with. Within those prison walls, there was tremendous racial tension.

The Federal Corrections Facility of Tucson is not the kind of environment that most CEO's of large corporations in America would do well in, let alone survive. Charlie Keating not only survived, he befriended nearly everyone there. Not unlike the banker that Tim Robbins portrayed in

The Shawshank Redemption, Charlie Keating became a kind of folk hero in the prison.

One day he sent one of his many inmate friends, an Hispanic he called *Irish,* who was incarcerated for manslaughter, to our home in Paradise Valley to stay with us upon being released after over twenty years. What a surprise it was when *Irish* showed up at our doorstep unannounced, with an *indefinite-welcome-pass* from my father-in-law. *Irish* stayed with us for months and got along well with all of us. My three sons particularly liked looking at the naked women tattooed on his body.

Charlie Keating was able to befriend prisoners, Hispanics, African Americans, Irish, or any race or color, because he started life with nothing. He learned to get along with everyone from an early age. It served him well in life and it served him well in prison.

One of the few times his life felt endangered in prison was when he walked into the television room in 1996 and changed the channel from the live NFL broadcast to the live coverage of the Atlanta Olympic Games. For a moment, he gazed around the room at a bunch of big guys giving him a death stare. Then he nervously smiled at the crowd of inmates and explained that his grandson, Gary Hall, Jr, was about to swim against a Russian guy named Popov for the gold medal. Within seconds, Gary Jr had the biggest cheering section outside of Atlanta and Keating was off the hook.

Although he was exonerated of his crimes five years after his imprisonment, virtually no one knows or recalls that Charlie Keating was not the S & L villain the media made him out to be. The financial losses that Lincoln Savings and Loan sustained as result of the takeover were mostly a result of the Resolution Trust Corporation, the bureaucratic arm of the Federal Home Loan Bank Board, selling off all of its assets for roughly ten cents on the dollar of their true worth. Lincoln's real estate assets were not like pieces of raw desert land of little value, as the media might have you think, but gems like the five-star Phoenician Resort and the beautifully developed Estrella Mountain Ranch properties. All assets were sold off cheaply by the government and enrichened those that virtually stole them from the RTC, resulting in losses recorded at $2.6 billion. Keating took the blame.

Instead, today, to those that remember him, Charlie Keating still remains a symbol of greed. His name is mentioned in the same breath along with Bernie Madoff. He never recovered financially from the indictment, dying penniless at the age of 90 in Arizona.

In 1999, just two years after his grandfather was released from prison, Gary Jr was diagnosed with Type 1 Diabetes. The first two Endocrinologists who treated Gary Jr gave him no chance of making his second Olympic Team of 2000, or any year after that. They considered that his athletic career was over. That was not the answer Gary Jr wanted to hear.

He sought another opinion from Dr. Anne Peters, a Diabetes specialist at UCLA, who told him she would help him try. That is all Gary needed to hear. With the help and supervision of Dr. Peters, Gary went on to win six more

Olympic medals at the Olympic Games of 2000 and 2004 with Type 1 Diabetes. That was brave.

In every single Olympic race that Gary Jr competed, he swam with his grandfather on his mind. Of his 10 Olympic medals -- 5 gold, 3 silver and 2 bronze -- six of them were earned with Type 1 Diabetes, including his two individual Olympic gold medals. By winning the Olympic races, Gary Jr demonstrated the same type of bravery that his grandfather had to face through his imprisonment. He also has inspired thousands of young, newly-diagnosed Diabetics to achieve just about anything they want, while faced with this incurable disease.

Shark Attack

When not training or teaching people how to swim faster or better, most of the Hall family loves spearfishing. While in the Florida Keys in 2006, training to try to qualify for his fourth Olympic Games, Gary Jr decided to take his sister, Bebe, out on our boat for a spearfishing excursion. Gary was 32 and Bebe was 28 years old at the time. Both were very experienced and capable of spearfishing.

Near Molasses Reef in about 30 feet of water, Gary spotted a large Mutton Snapper and immediately dove down for the chase. Against Gary's strong kick and deadly aim, even a Mutton Snapper didn't stand much of a chance. Gary's pinpoint accuracy from about 6 feet away resulted in the Snapper wiggling fiercely from the end of his spear. While clutching his Hawaiian sling, he quickly grabbed the end of the spear with the heavy fish dangling on the other end, held in place by a metal flange on the other side of the spear.

By the time he surfaced and looked around to spot the boat anchored nearby, he realized that he had ventured about 200 yards away from it in pursuit of this prize fish. Bebe, observing the chase from the surface above, reconnected with Gary after he broke the surface.

"Nice shot!" she proclaimed. "Let's get it back to the boat."

Gary started kicking on his back, holding the fish above the water, fresh blood dripping from its wound as it wiggled fiercely to try to free itself from the spear. Knowing the blood was leaving a nice scent trail behind them, Bebe kept watch underwater for unwanted sharks as they made their way toward the boat.

About half way back, she spotted a four or five foot black-tipped reef shark circling Gary Jr and moving in closer to the fish.

"Gary!!!" she screamed at him. "There is a small reef shark circling you! Be careful!"

Gary stuck his mask underwater and spotted the shark circling closer. He continued holding the heavy fish above the water as well as he could, but now kicked on his side, keeping a watchful eye on the circling shark. They were still not near the boat.

Suddenly, Bebe felt a blunt thump on her right arm. She turned quickly, thinking that she had run into Gary. Rather than finding her brother, she discovered a second, larger black-tipped shark swimming next to her. Blood was oozing from her right upper arm.

By the time she popped her head out of the water to inform Gary that she had been bitten, the shark was now viciously thrashing between Gary's legs, trying desperately to get to the speared fish. Gary immediately let go of the fish and the spear and let them sink together to the bottom. Undeterred, the shark continued thrashing between Gary's legs. He started punching the shark with his fists while it continued thrashing around. Miraculously, Gary did not get bitten during the short, violent frenzy.

When the shark finally swam away from between Gary's legs, it turned quickly toward her with its jaw wide open. It was in full attack mode, swimming at full speed. Bebe had a flash of an instant to react. There was not even time to think.

With his spear now on the bottom of the ocean, Gary was unarmed and helpless. Bebe clutched her spear and sling strongly. With the spear in one hand, she pulled back on the sling with her other hand as far as her strength would enable her. When the shark was about a foot away from her, she let the spear go right into the mouth of the shark. It lodged somewhere in the throat of the shark.

The shark aborted its attack on Bebe and began shaking its mouth trying to release the spear, just a few feet away from her. Knowing it was their only remaining spear, Bebe immediately grabbed the end of her spear, protruding from the shark's mouth. With a tremendous tug, she yanked the spear out of the shark's mouth. The shark, deciding that there were easier meals to get, swam away with blood trailing from its mouth.

Back in the boat, Gary used a sling rubber band to form a tourniquet around Bebe's arm to stop the bleeding. He called me immediately to explain what happened. Not knowing the extent of her injury, I nervously waited for them at the nearest dock. Upon arrival, I drove Bebe to the Emergency Room at Mariner's Hospital in Tavernier where she received excellent care. It required 19 stitches to close her three wounds, left from the razor-sharp teeth of the shark. It took Bebe's incredible bravery to save them both from a much worse outcome.

In life, you will be called on to be brave at some time and place. You need to be brave in your own way and at the right time. Take a lesson from Bebe and Gary Jr.

- **When it is your time to be brave, be brave.**

Lesson Nine
On raising future Olympians

"It's not whether you get knocked down: it's whether you get up." – Vince Lombardi

Some of the most common personality traits of Olympians are the same ones that can get them, or anyone else, in trouble. Dogged determination, strong will, stubbornness, aggression, defiance, killer instinct…just to name a few. As parents, when we observe our children demonstrating these or other similar personality traits, we are not sure whether to applaud them or reprimand them. Most of the time, it is much better to applaud.

While nice guys may not always finish last, the truth is that on the starting blocks, Olympic gold medalists transform into killers. To win, they have to be. They are either born that way, or they become that way, but regardless, on the *killer instinct* scale, they rate 10/10.

The world is a tough place. To some extent, it will always be *survival of the fittest*. At some point, in order to succeed, we all need to increase our *killer instinct* rating. In our Race Club camps, these are the five points we teach our swimmers how to improve on their *killer instinct* scale:

1. **Set Goals**. Goals should be set not only for the near future, but also written and placed somewhere where you can see them every day. Set your goals as specifically as you can.

2. **Visualize**. See yourself achieving your goals from beginning to end. In sports, we have our athletes visualize themselves performing their sport vividly and perfectly in their minds...every week.
3. **Confidence**. Build confidence by adhering to your plan, testing yourself and correcting your mistakes. Perfection can never be reached, but the process of getting closer to it is well defined.
4. **Focus.** It is easy to get distracted from your goals or your mission. Warren Buffett and Bill Gates both singled out their ability to *focus* as the single most important quality that led to their successes.
5. **Anchor.** When it is time to perform, you must do something that triggers your mind, letting you know that you are now ready for action. It is the final important step in your climb up on the *killer instinct* scale.

Whether in business, art, music, sports, politics or any other endeavor, the greatest over-achievers, the Olympic gold medalists, have more than talent. They are driven way beyond others. The origin of their extraordinary drive is often rooted in their childhood. It is typically not something pleasant, but rather a bomb that went off.

It may have been an absent or abusive parent, an imprisoned member of the family or someone that caused embarrassment to the family name, or a death or severe illness in the family. Whatever it was, it was severe, and it caused a commitment of the child to rise from the ashes, to climb above all others. This horrible event or situation resulted in an incredible *killer instinct,* will and an ability to work extremely hard to be able to win at whatever the game being played.

The likelihood of a child that participates in any Olympic sport actually making the Olympic Team is about 1 per 10,000 athletes. The chance of winning an Olympic gold medal is roughly one in a million athletes. While making your country's Olympic Team is something to be extremely proud of, and winning a medal even more so, the real value of sports is what is learned and gained in the journey.

If making the Olympic Team was the only prize or benefit, we'd find just one happy athlete out of 10,000 in each sport. We don't. Instead, we find that most of the 9,999 other athletes who didn't make the Olympic Team loved the journey and learned a lot from it. The Olympic Games may have taught me a lot, but I learned most of the lessons about life on the journey there.

I don't think that Mary and I did anything special to end up with our oldest son becoming an Olympic Champion. In fact, Gary Jr's grandfather probably had more to do with it than we did. We were just part of his supporting cast.

In 1989 Charlie Keating built an Olympic pool and grass training track in central Phoenix, called the Phoenix Swim Club. It would become a source of millions of dollars of athletic scholarships that were awarded to hundreds of young swimmers that trained there for more than a decade. It served countless others for learning to swim and exercise. Keating had already done the same thing once in Cincinnati on the campus of St. Xavier High School. He knew how much value the pools brought to the community, so he did it again in Phoenix.[12]

Charlie Keating was once an NCAA champion swimmer in 1946, defeating another swimmer named James Counsilman in the finals of the 200 yard breaststroke at Yale University. If he had not later joined the Navy, Keating would have had a good chance of making the 1948 Olympic Team in London. By that time both swimmers had moved on.

Counsilman pursued his studies in Iowa, earning a PhD in physiology, and then went on to become the greatest swimming coach in history at Indiana University. He was known as the *father of swimming science*. Keating went to law school, established one of the most successful law firms in Cincinnati, Keating, Muething and Klekamp, and eventually turned to business. They remained lifelong friends, both passionate about swimming.

1989 was also the year that the bomb dropped in Charlie Keating's life. The RTC took over all of the properties of Lincoln Savings, including the Phoenix Swim Club. Once the RTC got a hold of it, they immediately shut it down.

For nearly two years, while the RTC held the property, the pools (there were two) and track remained closed, with a 24-hour security guard sitting in front. The water in the pools turned dark green from algae growing, and all of the

---

[12] The Phoenix Swim Club was eventually purchased by Brophy College Preparatory School. Years later, the property was sold to a home builder and the facilities were rebuilt on the campus of the school.

pool equipment rotted away from hot sun and neglect. Charlie Keating was sent to prison.

Finally, with the help of the Crean Family Foundation in Orange County, California, where I had grown up, we were able to purchase the facility back from the RTC at 15% of its original cost. It became part of the $2.6 billion of lost value attributed to Keating's so-thought *inept* running of Lincoln S & L. For Gary Jr, that purchase came none too soon.

Within a few weeks, we had the pools and track cleaned up and running again. The young swimming members of the Phoenix Swim Club, including 16-year-old Gary Jr, were back working out. While Gary may have had some of the Olympic personality traits, we certainly didn't recognize too many of them. Most of his free time was spent honing his skateboarding skills, listening to music or playing video games. He liked sports, but never pursued any of them with enough effort, time or passion to reach a high level. He was a free-spirited kid that seemed an unlikely candidate to become an Olympic Champion.

Sixteen is also an extremely late age to be starting out on a successful swimming career. Gary Jr was no ordinary swimmer, in any sense of the word. Beneath the surface of a free-spirited and defiant teenaged kid, was an incredible natural swimmer. Normally, Gary was somewhat apathetic about racing, often coming in dead last in competitions. Mary and I didn't know if it was because of lack of talent or interest or both. We had just accepted that fact that he was not going to be a great swimmer, until that day in the high school Championship meet before his grandfather went off to prison. That is when we saw the *killer instinct* in him for the first time.

From there, Gary kept getting better and better. The better he got, the more he loved the sport. Throughout his career, he remained well outside the box, never quite going by the book. His training, his philosophy and his approach were all outside the norm. He took great pride in that, even though many of the top coaches did not like him for it.

For Gary Jr it was never about the medals or the records. It was always about the race. He loved the race. Defiant at times, but perhaps no race in his career defined him more than his final Olympic race in Athens in 2004.

The Ready Room in Athens

By the time the day arrived for the men's 50-meter sprint late in the week of Olympic swimming competition, Gary was angry. The coaches' decision to leave him off the final team of the 4 x 100 freestyle relay on the first day did not sit well with him. Not unexpectedly, Michael Phelps was anointed to the relay, even though he hadn't swum the 100 freestyle final at the Trials. It was the coaches' prerogative to do so. That meant one of the other freestylers would have to be taken off the relay. It was not an easy call. They chose Gary.

What made it worse for Gary is that the American team did not do well in the finals, placing third. The leadoff swimmer, Ian Crocker, had a bad swim and they never got back in the race. Gary felt he could have made a difference in the outcome, but we will never know.

The day after that relay, Gary went missing in Athens. He felt like he had to get away. No one knew where he was or what he was up to. There were three days remaining before he would be swimming in his only individual event, the 50 meter freestyle. Even so, he was expected to be there to cheer for the team. Yet, he was nowhere to be found. Mary and I had no idea of his whereabouts, either.

Gary had taken a taxi to the nearby port and jumped on a hydrofoil boat over to the nearest Greek Island of Hydra. There, he had lunch, walked around and cleared his head. By that evening, after a cooling off period, he returned to Athens and the Olympic Village to rejoin the Team. He missed the finals competition, however. The coaches were not happy.

In fact, they were so concerned about Gary that they had one of the Team managers, Everett Uchiyama, trail him, making sure that he obeyed the Team orders. For the next two days, he followed Gary everywhere like a puppy dog, even into the bathroom. It was annoying, but Gary put up with it.

On August 19, the day of the men's 50 meter freestyle preliminaries and semi-finals, both Americans, Gary and Jason Lezak, made it through to the finals. Lezak qualified 3rd and Gary 5th for the finals the following night. Only .2 seconds separated the fastest qualifier, Roland Schoeman from South Africa, from the 8th qualifier from Croatia, Duje Draganja. Anyone in the finals could win. Gary cooperated, doing everything that he was supposed to do in the heats and semifinals, wearing the Nike warmups and Speedo trunks, fitting in nicely with the rest of the Team.

On the evening of August 20, the finals for the men's 50 meter freestyle, the coaches were concerned about Gary Jr In the Olympic Trials, Gary paraded up to the blocks wearing a long, red, white and blue Everlast boxing robe and boxing trunks, just like Apollo Creed wore in the Rocky movies. Then, standing behind the blocks, when they announced his name, Gary went into his customary shadow boxing routine. It was his pre-race ritual and *anchor* that he had become well-known for doing.

It wasn't the boxing the coaches were worried about, it was the robe. It wasn't a Nike robe and it wasn't part of the Team uniform. Nike had paid the USOC handsomely to require all the athletes to wear their warmups. The athletes did not get paid to do so.

Just to be safe, the coaches asked Everett to tail Gary closer than ever and even to confront him about the robe. Everett asked Gary specifically if he was planning on wearing the boxing robe to the finals. He shook his head, no.

To Gary, the boxing robe and shorts were part of his persona. As far as he was concerned, they were an essential part of his mental preparation. He actually didn't think he could win without them. When they called the eight men sprinters to the ready room for the finals, the small room where they gathered before being paraded to the starting blocks, Gary had made up his mind.

Wearing his gray USA Nike warmups with his towel rolled up under his right arm, Gary walked toward the ready room. Everett was two steps behind him. When they reached the door to the ready room, there were two big guards standing outside of the room, making sure that only the eight finalists entered. No one else was allowed in. When Gary passed through the door into the room, Everett was stopped by the guards.

By the time Gary arrived, several of the other finalists were already seated in the room. He was one of the last to arrive. He sat down in his chair, marked with Lane 2, among the other athletes. He then took his towel and placed it down on the concrete floor and unrolled it. Rolled up inside the towel was his bright red, white and blue Everlast boxing robe, printed with stars and stripes. He took off his warmups and underneath he was wearing his red, white and blue boxing shorts.

Everett watched as this happened and started screaming, "Gary!!!!"

His face turned bright red. The veins of his neck were popping out. He tried to get through the door but was restrained by the guards.

He kept screaming, "You said you wouldn't wear the robe!!" Finally, they carried Everett away, as he continued screaming.

Every swimmer's attention in the room was immediately diverted to the commotion. Gary did not intend for the explosion to become a distraction, but that is what happened. The robe was really just about getting Gary ready, not about distracting the others.

Soon, the eight finalists were marching to the starting blocks to music, following the lead woman carrying the placard stating *Men's 50 meter Freestyle Final.* Gary's long red, white and blue robe flowed behind him gracefully toward the ground. Open in the front, his matching Everlast boxing shorts hung down nearly to his knees, emblazoned on the white waistband with his name *Gary Hall Jr* in big red letters. A black Team USA racing cap, with his name and the American flag printed on both sides, covered his head. His small racing goggles with mirrored surfaces covered his eyes.

On the swimmer's parade toward the starting block, television announcer Dan Hicks commented to his Olympian expert sidekick, Rowdy Gaines.

"He's not supposed to be wearing that robe, is he?" he asked.

Rowdy laughed and said, "That's Gary Hall Jr."

Upon being introduced to the crowd of around 10,000 spectators, while wearing the boxing robe and shorts, Gary momentarily stopped shaking his arms and raised them both overhead. Then clasping both hands together, he elevated his arms back up above his head first to one side, then to the other. It is known as the *Victory Clasp.* Few athletes are bold enough to proclaim victory before the event is competed. Gary Jr had that kind of confidence, especially with the robe on. Even at the Olympic Games.

The start was clean. No one had a bad start, which would have ruined his race. As expected, Roland Schoeman, one of the greatest starters in the world, broke out slightly ahead of the rest of the field. Mary and I were sitting around the midway point down the pool, about half way up. Gary, in Lane 2, was closest to our side of the pool. We had a great view of the race.

By the time the swimmers passed us, there was one continuous wall of water from the eight massive swimmers powering their way down the pool. It was impossible to tell who would win. It was that close. Mary and I were holding our breath, our hearts pounding nearly as fast as Gary Jr's was. With only about 12 seconds left in the race, it would be over in a few blinks of the eyes.

Just passed the midway point, I remember yelling out, "He's got it!"

In reviewing the videos of the race later, I had no right to say that at that moment. It was just an instinctive response, a father's wishful thinking. But I knew Gary always finished this race fast.

When the swimmers were just outside the backstroke flags, some five meters to the wall, Gary took a breath. My heart almost stopped. Most 50 meter sprinters don't breathe during the entire race, but Gary usually would took one breath. But why now? So close to the wall? Taking a breath always momentarily slows a swimmer down, yet at around 20 seconds into a race that oxygen becomes crucial. This race would last just less than 22 seconds.

108

After putting his head down after the breath, Gary took exactly four strokes to the finish, reaching out with his long arms to drive his hand firmly to the wall. They were four of the fastest strokes I had ever seen him take. We turned back and looked up at the giant scoreboard at the starting end of the pool, still uncertain of the outcome. There was his name with a number 1 next to it and his time of 21.93, exactly .01 seconds ahead of the second-place swimmer, Draganje, from Croatia.

Gary jumped out of the pool and raised his arms in celebration for the second time in less than five minutes. Then, he waited at the side of the pool as each swimmer in the race climbed out, shaking each of their hands, hugging some. Win or lose, Gary always did the same thing. He was a good sport.

For his defiance, Gary Jr was fined $5,000 by the USOC for not wearing the Team uniform. He gladly paid it. He has since told me several times that he would not have won that race without the robe. The fine was worth every penny.

As parents, we sometimes suppress or quash the very qualities of our children that can help them become gold medalists, or simply better competitors in life. If you have a strong-willed child that may be stubborn, determined, or even defiant at times, embrace it. It is a blessing, not a curse. Help to channel your child's energy and drive in the right direction. You never know where it may lead to.

- **As for what to tell your children before they engage in battle of any sort, there are two words** that work extremely well. It is the only advice I gave Gary Jr before each and every important race of his career -- *have fun*. At that crucial time, those words are all that are needed to be said.

- At the completion of each battle, win or lose, there are three words that work equally well. In fact, they are the three most powerful words in the English language -- *I love you*. If you add a hug, they become even more meaningful. Those words say it all, if you really mean them.

Lesson Ten
Today you are on the podium

"Human greatness does not lie in wealth or power, but in character and goodness. People are just people, and all people have faults and shortcomings, but all of us are born with a basic goodness." - Anne Frank

Standing on the Olympic podium with your National Anthem being played while your flag is being raised..... well, that is a pretty special feeling. It doesn't get much better, except when you get to watch your son or daughter on the podium in the same place. That is as good as it gets.

Imagine how you would feel if today you were to have the gold medal draped around your neck, while the National Anthem is played and the entire world looked on and applauded your life's accomplishments with a standing ovation. I would think that would put you in a pretty good mood. You would feel very good about yourself.

Of course, the award ceremony for your life's accomplishments will never happen in any official capacity. The world will certainly not be there to watch nor applaud. The point is that if we can feel so good about what we have done in our lifetime on a given day, why can't we feel that way every day? Our lifetime is simply made up of lots of one days.

"Well, they can't all be good days", you are probably thinking.

Actually, they can be. Every day of your life is what you make it out to be. Even those days when the bomb drops. It is all about attitude. Your daily attitude is often determined by the way in which you start your day.

At night, when you go to bed, you may be preoccupied with your struggles. You may be thinking about your business, your credit card debt, your sick child or family member, your fight with your spouse, or hundreds of other potential problems. Whatever the concerns are, they make you toss and turn and toss again, until you finally fall asleep from sheer exhaustion.

When the alarm goes off the next morning, and you are all glassy-eyed from not having slept well, you start right back in where you left off the previous night, remembering life's problems. It is very difficult to focus on solutions when you are consumed by problems.

No wonder you start off each day in a bad mood. No wonder you are grumpy and irritable most of the time. When you focus most of your time and attention worrying about your life's problems, how can you expect to be in anything other than a bad mood? You can't.

Many years ago, in my Ophthalmology practice, long before cell phones, I met a patient in my office named Gus. When I walked into the exam room, he was holding a small, handheld device and reading his emails. Everyone else at the time was getting emails on their desktop computers. I was intrigued by this device, one of the first that Blackberry manufactured.

Before I even had a chance to examine his eyes, he was already explaining what the device was and describing his new company, NetSearch. Recently, he had tried to buy a car online, since he hated going to car dealerships. Not one dealership called him back right away, so he decided there had to be a market for that software; to help customers buy cars less painfully. He patented his idea, started NetSearch and set out to change the world.

I don't know why, but I instinctively trusted this guy, so I invested a few dollars in NetSearch. It turned out to be one of the better investments I have made in my life. Eighteen months after founding NetSearch, precisely one month before the dot-com crash, and before NetSearch ever made one dime of profit, Gus sold the company for $60 million in cash. Six months later, NetSearch was out of business.

Gus has a very positive outlook on life. Unquestionably, he made the deal happen because he willed it to happen. His whole attitude about life was exemplified by the message on his cell phone. I used to call him occasionally, hoping he wouldn't answer the phone, just so I could hear the message. It was as if I needed to hear it.

"Hi, this is Gus. I'm sorry I'm not available to answer your call, but I do promise I will get back to you right away. Leave me a message and, by the way, I hope today is one of the best days of your life."

That simple message seemed to change my whole outlook on the day's events. It would take my focus away from my problems and make me remember that life really is good. It made me feel so much better, that I finally decided that I didn't need to call Gus and hope he didn't answer his phone in order to get that message. I could do it myself. I decided to convert that phone message into a short thought or a prayer to start my day.

Since then, each morning in the shower, I don't think about my problems. Instead, I start my day with this simple thought, *"God, please help make today one of the best days of my life."*

By saying that little thought or prayer, it creates an attitude that makes the day much easier to get through. That prayer plants a message in my subconscious that tells me I can deal with whatever problems confront me that day. That prayer makes the glass look half full, instead of half empty. It gives me an inner strength that is much greater than I would have had without it. It makes me smile instead of frown.

When I was four years old, my grandmother was already in her 90's. Twice a year, for the few years remaining in her life, she would come to our home for Thanksgiving and Christmas dinner. She was in a wheel chair and didn't remember my name. She didn't even remember my father's name. They didn't call it Alzheimer's disease back then. My father just said she was *senile*.

When she arrived, my mother would make me go up to her and stand on my tiptoes and give her a kiss on the cheek. She had a big mole on one side with hair growing out of it, so I would always pick the other cheek. Even so, I always dreaded that moment.

After giving her that kiss twice a year for a few years, although she didn't remember my name nor know who I was, I began to observe something in my grandmother. Each time I would kiss her, a big smile would break out on her face. I could almost begin to feel her mood change.

I have never forgotten how that little kiss on her cheek affected her. In my 24-year career as an Ophthalmologist, for the older women patients that came to my office, I adopted that same custom my mother taught me. I would greet each woman with a kiss on the cheek when I came into the exam room. Why? I soon learned from my practice that the most common disease in America is not glaucoma or cataract. It is not even heart disease or cancer. It is loneliness.

Just as it had for my grandmother, each time I would plant a little kiss on the cheek of my patients, I could feel their warmth. And they could feel mine. For many of them, it may have been the first kiss they'd had since, well, the last time they were in my office. And just like with my grandmother, a subtle little smile would usually break out from that kiss. Sometimes, patients would return to the office at 3 months, instead of their scheduled 6-month visit, just because they needed that kiss.

Of course, they wouldn't say so, but I began to see that the kiss was helping them heal. It was helping to cure their eye disease, their heart disease, their cancer and most importantly, their loneliness.

Loneliness doesn't necessarily come from being alone. Some people can be blanketed by others around them, yet still feel alone, because they never feel the warmth. They are not connected. People can have big families and still be lonely. People can be young and still be lonely. The fact is people need to be hugged and kissed. They need to feel loved.

When he was in late 70's, Warren Buffett, among the richest people on earth and arguably the smartest investor of all time, had this to say about life's success:

"Basically, when you get to be my age you will measure your success in life by how many of the people you want to have love you actually do love you....
...The trouble with love is that you cannot buy it. You can buy sex. You can buy testimonial dinners. You can buy pamphlets that say how wonderful you are. But the only way to get love is to be loveable. It is very irritating if you have a lot of money. You'd like to think that you can write a check: I'll buy a million dollars' worth of love. But it doesn't work that way. The more you give love away, the more you get."[13]

The reason you need to know this is that it is very hard to prescribe or give when you are depressed or angry. If you are consumed with your life's problems, you will not feel like giving out hugs and kisses. You won't feel like saying "I love you." The truth is you need love just as much as the people around you do, maybe even more.

---

[13] Schroeder, Alice. *The Snowball* Warren Buffett and the Business of Life, Bantam Books 2008.

Circle of Life

Standing in line at the airport in Munich in 1972, toward the end of the Olympic Games, waiting to catch a flight to Vienna, I was depressed. The terrorist attack was a nightmare and I could not get the thought of losing the 400 IM out of my mind. To make matters worse, I was standing in line right behind Steve Prefontaine, America's greatest distance runner of the time. *Pre,* as he was called, was also dejected about not medaling in the 5000 meter run in Munich. He was hoping to possibly win, yet he came in fourth, just out of the medals.

All *Pre* talked about in line was the Olympic Games of Montreal in 1976; how he would come back, faster than ever, and win the gold medal for the USA. Unknowingly, he was making me even sadder. Not only had I let America down, I thought there would be no more Olympic Games in my future. I was to enter medical school the following year, get married, and there would be no more time in my life left for training. My sprint phase of life was ending and the pentathlon phase beginning.

After getting his boarding pass, *Pre* went off to catch his flight back to Oregon. It was the last time I would ever see him. Tragically, in May 1975, just a year before Montreal, *Pre* was killed in a car accident. He never got his *do-over.*

I was flying to Vienna as a favor to a man I ran into in Munich. His name was Mr. Rexa and was from Bratislava, Czechoslovakia. He organized a swimming meet each year called the *Slovakian Grand Prix,* where I had competed a few years earlier. In Munich, he asked me if I would come back and compete again after the Olympic swimming competition ended. He had treated me well, so I agreed.

The flight to Vienna and drive to Bratislava, just 30 minutes away by car, were really just a stop-over on my way to Athens. From there, I would fly to the Island of Crete for a few days of vacation; time to decompress. I agreed to swim in Bratislava for just one day.

Re-entering Bratislava reminded me of how oppressed and poor the people of this Communist country were. It hadn't changed at all since I was last here. People were sad and depressed. The city was gray. The pool was drab and falling apart. I was glad I was not staying long.

I swam two events that day in Bratislava, enough to satisfy Mr. Rexa. The times were not fast, but he didn't care. Nor did I care. He appreciated that I had come to the meet. After completing the second event, I threw on my warmups, grabbed my swimming bag and headed for the exit, anxious to catch a cab to the airport in Vienna.

Just as I was about to head out the door, a young 14-year old Slovakian boy came up to me with his older sister. He didn't speak English well, so he tugged on my warmup sleeve. I turned and saw a poor young swimmer, staring up at me, unsure of what to tell me. He turned to his sister who spoke some English.

"My brother wants to know if he can have your shirt?" she asked.

The t-shirt I was wearing beneath my warmups was an official USA Olympic Team shirt, with the five Olympic rings printed on the front. Each athlete received only four of them and they were coveted by all. If I were to give him the one I was wearing, I doubted I could get another one. My first instinct was to tell him *no*.

Then I gazed down again into his eyes. I could see how badly he wanted it; how much it would mean to him. It took a lot of courage for him to even ask me for it. People in Bratislava at that time had very little to smile about.

I dropped my swimming bag to the ground, pulled off my warmup top, took off the t-shirt and handed it to him. A big smile broke across his face. He said *thankyou* in his broken English and walked away beaming. I didn't even catch his name.

I put my warmup top back on, grabbed my bag and headed for the airport. I never thought about that t-shirt again......until 45 years later.

After my Navy Seal nephew, Charlie Keating IV, was killed in Iraq in 2016, and Mary and I attended his Ceremony in Coronado, California, we made a big decision. We would start a Race Club operation on the West Coast in Coronado, along with our Florida Keys operation.

Two of Mary's siblings lived in Coronado with their children, so being close to family had much to do with our decision to start a second location. Another one of my nephews, Bobby Wurzelbacher, worked in Coronado for a real estate company. Not long after Mary and I rented a home in Coronado for us and her 90-year-old mother, Bobby came up to me one day.

"My boss is Pieter Zajac. His father, Anton, says that he knows you", he said. "Does that name sound familiar?"

"Not really", I responded. "From where?"

"His family lives outside of Vienna", he continued. "They invited me over there last year and when we went for a swim in a nearby lake, Anton challenged me to a swimming race. He said he used to swim competitively."

Bobby had been an excellent competitive swimmer on the Phoenix Swim Club growing up, so he managed to win the race against Anton handily. Anton asked him where he learned to swim so fast.

"I grew up with a family of swimmers", he explained to Anton. "Both my cousin and my uncles were Olympians."

"Oh yea," Anton responded. "What are their names?"

"Gary Hall Jr and Gary Hall Sr."

Anton's jaw dropped open. His mind raced back to that day in Bratislava where I had gifted him my Olympic t-shirt. He couldn't believe Bobby was related to us. He proceeded to tell Bobby the whole story of that day in Bratislava.

Anton never excelled as a swimmer. He was a brilliant student, however. He studied math and physics in school. A year after we met, he broke his back and was confined to bed rest for almost six months. That ended his competitive swimming career. During that time, he read every book on chess that he could find. When he was released from the hospital, he entered and won the National Chess Championship of Czechoslovakia, even though he had never played a match with anyone in his life. He was fifteen years old. That is how brilliant he is.

To Anton, the Olympic shirt was not just a collector's item. It became a symbol - a source of inspiration. If he were not to become an Olympic swimmer, he was going to become a gold medalist in something. He would work his way out of the Communist regime of Czechoslovakia.

Anton wore that Olympic shirt nearly every day for years. Finally, his mother tried to bleach out a stain on the front of the shirt and caused a hole to form, instead. Anton was devastated. From that day on, he would need to live with the memory of that shirt.

After finishing school, Anton used his newly acquired skills in computer science to develop and patent a cyber-security system that would become the most secure system in the world. His idea was to build a virtual computer that would serve as a firewall to protect all incoming information. Then, if anything unwanted would filter through the virtual computer, the second security system in the company's main computers would catch it. He founded a company, called ESET, that grew to become the fourth largest cyber-security company in the world, doing business in over 70 countries. His clients include Microsoft, Apple and many countries around the world. He now has a home outside Vienna and another in Coronado. He swims almost every day for exercise and stress relief.

Anton and I met for the second time in 45 years on the pool deck in Coronado a few months later for a swimming workout. We hugged. The tears welled up in his eyes as he explained how much that shirt had meant to him. It was what drove him to become successful.

The following year, Anton invited Gary Jr and his son, Charlie, Mary and me to come to Vienna for the dedication of his new ten-million-dollar Olympic natatorium. He named it the *Gary Hall Swimming Center*.

From a small, spontaneous act of kindness that meant so little to me at the time, came a dream and an ambition so great, it changed the world for the better. I am honored to be Anton's friend.

Every small gift, act of kindness or amount of love you can give will come back to help you in some way. That is why it is so important to start out each day with that little thought or prayer that Gus taught me. That simple little prayer will put you in the frame of mind to prescribe love. It will not only help you get through the day, but it will help others around you get through their day, too. That little prayer, believe it or not, will make your life a lot more fun. It will make you a better pentathlete.

- **Get rid of your anger. Get rid of your depression. Start smiling. Today you are on the podium.**

The Closing Ceremony

"How wonderful it is that nobody need wait a single moment before starting to improve the world." Anne Frank

At the 1984 Olympics in Los Angeles, I sat with Gary Jr in the stands for the finals of the swimming competition. He was just ten years old. I loved the Olympic Games and still do. The entire city was filled with excitement. Amidst the pin trading, national pride, flag waving and pageantry, new heroes were emerging every single day. Mary Lou Retton, Carl Lewis, Michael Jordan....who would become the latest hero?

It is true. I was hoping that at such a young, impressionable age, Gary would catch a bit of the Olympic fever. He hadn't even started swimming yet, but I had hopes. What Olympian father wouldn't?

It was a good time for us. Business was good. We were affluent enough to afford front row seats at the Olympic venues and limousine rides to and from the Beverly Wilshire to catch the events. It was a patriotic moment. There was a lot to smile about.

In the finals of the men's 200 meters backstroke, Rick Carey, an American, was the clear favorite to win the gold medal. He was the World Record holder and before the event, he had boldly predicted that he would not only win the gold medal, but would also shatter his World Record.

Well, Rick did win the gold, as he predicted, but he failed to break his own World Record. His winning time was slower than he had swum in the preliminaries. After the medals were presented to the three swimmers at the awards ceremony, they paraded around the pool. The two swimmers from France and Canada that won the silver and bronze medals were smiling jubilantly, waving to the crowd and laughing. They were having fun. Rick walked around the pool hangdogging it, like he had just had a bad day at the office. There were no smiles, no waves to the crowd; no appearance of joy, whatsoever.

Rick was such a fierce competitor, he allowed the disappointment of not breaking his own World Record exceed the thrill of winning an Olympic gold medal. He may not have even been aware of his emotions at the time. Many of the young people of the world watching him were.

As the athletes passed in front of us, Gary turned toward me with a puzzled look and asked, "Dad, didn't he just win the gold medal? Why is he so sad?"

I thought for a moment and realized I couldn't come up with a good answer. "I don't know, Gary," I said. "I'm not really sure."

In life, it seems as if there are those who smile a lot and those who don't. There are those who see life as something beautiful and others who view it as morbid. There are those who know how to make lemonade out of lemons and those who never try. There are those who, no matter what the challenges and the obstacles, somehow manage to see that life is good; that it is truly worth living.

I am glad that I am not a judge of anyone's life, but if I were, I would probably award the gold medals to those people who have done well in all five events in their lives: family, faith, profession, community and health. I would give extra bonus points to those who have spent a good portion of their lives smiling. Smiling is so contagious. It has the power to heal emotionally and physically.

I would also reward those who have had the ability and the courage to say *I love you* and *I'm sorry* or *forgive me* because they are among the most powerful words in the English language. God is willing to forgive us, so we should be willing to forgive each other. We should be willing to forgive ourselves. At the right time and for the right reasons, saying those short sentences can mean everything. Those words also have the ability to heal. They can make the world a better place.

This has been my lesson book for winning life's gold medal. What is at stake, however, is much more than an imaginary medal or your pride. What is at stake is our country and the world.

In a world that is changing faster than ever before, some for the good and some for the bad, *making America great again* really starts with you making yourself great again. The greatest America will emerge when its people are great.

Whatever the sins of your past, you cannot completely erase your history any more than you can erase our country's history. Instead, you can learn from it. You can learn from the Olympic ideals. You can get better.

Don't worry about others who may judge you. To get better, become a judge of yourself. Judge yourself in the correct events: faith, family, profession, community and health. Do it often, like every week, not every year.

Start each day with a smile and a short, positive thought. Celebrate every victory and achievement you have, no matter how small. Help others to do the same. If you do that, and adjust your pentathlon training every week, you will be on your way to helping solve the world's problems.

However, please don't feel disappointed when at the end of your life, there is no podium, no medals, no audience to give you an ovation; not even the national anthem, whether you deserve it or not. The best you can really hope for is that in this split second of eternity we call *life*, you live each day to the fullest.

When you are in the sprint phase of life, then sprint. When you are in the pentathlon phase of life, become good, not necessarily great, in all five of life's events.

What is really important throughout your life is that you feel good about yourself. That even with all of life's turmoil, you are able to smile most of the time and help others around you smile, too. That makes life really special.

What you really want is for your family and friends, the people you really care about, the ones that really count, to say: *You know, if they ever give out gold medals for living life, you sure should win one.*

Then you can go to sleep, without tossing or turning.

About the Author

Gary Hall Sr has been involved in swimming for nearly his entire life. He rose to prominence quickly as a young competitive swimmer in Southern California, breaking 22 National Records by the age of ten. By 16, he qualified for his first of three Olympic Games of 1968, 1972 and 1976, where he earned three individual medals and was part of the gold medal winning medley relay team in 1972. He was twice voted as the Men's World Swimmer of the Year in 1969 and 1970. From 1969-1973 he attended Indiana University, swimming for legendary coach, James 'Doc' Counsilman. While there, he won seven individual NCAA titles and helped Indiana University win four consecutive team championships. Among his many honors, his greatest occurred during the 1976 Olympic Games, where he was selected by the Team Captains of all sports to carry the United States Flag, leading Team USA into the Opening Ceremony. He was the first American swimmer in history to receive that honor. Michael Phelps received the same honor in 2016.

After completing his swimming career, Gary finished medical school at University of Cincinnati. During medical school, he supported his family by coaching swimming at the well-known Cincinnati Marlins. After completing his Residency in Ophthalmology at Indiana University Medical Center, he practiced in Phoenix, Arizona until 2006. During his 24 years as an Ophthalmologist, Gary built a large practice, pioneered surgical procedures and performed clinical research. On the side, he managed the very successful Phoenix Swim Club and competed in triathlons and Masters swimming.

From 1996 to 2004, Gary proudly watched his son, Gary Jr, surpass his swimming accomplishments by winning ten Olympic medals in three Olympic Games. To this day, Gary Sr and Gary Jr are the only father and son in sports history to each compete in three Olympic Games.

In 2003, Gary Jr co-founded The Race Club in Islamorada, Florida, as a training program for aspiring Olympic swimmers. Gary Sr joined his son in this endeavor in 2006, moving to Florida from Arizona.

After he retired from competitive swimming in 2008, Gary Jr began to focus on finding the cure for Type I Diabetes, with which he was diagnosed in 1999. He has become one of the world's leading advocates for diabetic patients.

Gary Sr and his wife, Mary, transitioned The Race Club from a training program into a teaching program, which it has been ever since. Gary Sr recently authored a textbook on swimming technique, entitled *Fundamentals of Fast Swimming-How to Improve Your Swim Technique.*

Today, The Race Club coaches improve swimmers' technique in Islamorada, Florida and Coronado, California. Gary Sr's second son, Richard, joined The Race Club in 2010, becoming the video production manager. Richard's Race Club educational videos are widely acclaimed by swimmers and coaches worldwide, with over 15 million *You Tube* views. Thousands of swimmers, coaches and triathletes all over the world subscribe to The Race Club instructional videos at www.theraceclub.com.

Gary Sr proudly carries the USA Flag in the Opening Ceremony of the 1976 Olympic Games while Queen Elizabeth (standing above) observes (API photo)

Mary holds Gary Jr during the Opening Ceremony in Montreal as he watches his father carry the flag for Team USA

Gary Sr celebrates making his third Olympic Team in Long Beach in 1976 by hoisting Gary Jr above his head

Gary Sr shows off his trophy and medals at the Sammy Lee Swimming and Diving School in Anaheim, CA circa 1959, standing next to teammate Tommy McClain

Coach Doc Counsilman cracking a joke with Gary Sr after a swimming practice at Indiana University in 1972

Mark Spitz was one of the groomsmen at Gary Sr's wedding to Mary
Keating in June, 1973

Mary Keating was a beautiful bride on our wedding day of June 30, 1973

Gary Sr kisses his mother-in-law on the cheek after winning the National Championships in Cincinnati in 1975 while in medical school

The 1976 USA Olympic Swimming Team produced two of the greatest performances in Olympic history

The women's 4 x 100 freestyle relay Olympic victory may have been the most heroic swim ever in defeating the steroid-bolstered East German women's team. L-R Kim Peyton, Wendy Boglioli, Jill Sterkel and Shirley Babashoff

Gary Jr grew up in Phoenix Arizona and started developing his swimming talent in high school at the Phoenix Swim Club and Brophy College Prep

Gary Jr started flexing his muscles even before he had much muscle to flex

The Hall children in Paradise Valley, Arizona in 1986 with their parents. They were all swimming by the age of two

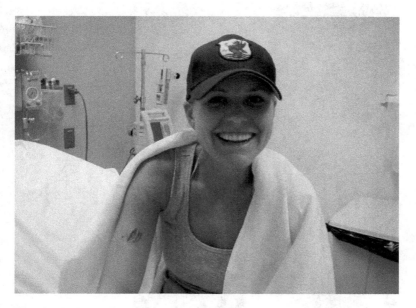

The shark bite on Bebe's arm could have been much worse, were it not for her bravery

Gary Jr getting ready to win the men's Olympic 50 meter freestyle in Athens 2004

Just under 22 seconds after starting the race and after a lifetime of preparation, Gary Jr celebrates his Olympic victory in the 50 meter freestyle sprint

Gary Jr and Gary Sr in Athens at the 2004 Olympic Games, celebrating his gold medal swim in the 50-meter sprint

Anton Zajac dedicated his Olympic Natatorium near Vienna to Gary Sr
for giving him his Olympic t-shirt in 1972

Gary Sr coaching a young swimmer at The Race Club on how to improve
her swimming technique

Even after spending nearly 5 years in prison, Charlie Keating Jr always
managed to smile